Confident Horse Foot Care using Reward Reinforcement

by Hertha James

Powerword Publications,

Muddy Horse Coaching

Palmerston North, New Zealand

hertha.james@xtra.co.nz

www.safehorse.info

www.herthamuddyhorse.com

Font: Bookman Old Style 11

Disclaimer of liability:

Horses that show dangerous behaviors should not be paired with casual or inexperienced horse owners or handlers. Readers are entirely in charge of their own actions.

Risk Radar: When around horses, we must have our Risk Radar on at all times.

Cover Photo: by Hertha James, featuring Smoky during a session filming saddle pads and sheets blowing in the wind.

Photography by: Bryan James, Hertha James and Bridget Evans unless otherwise noted. Some of the photos are taken from video footage, which decreases quality but allows illustration of an exact moment or exact movement.

With willing hearts and skilful hands, the difficult we do at once, the impossible takes a bit longer.

Author unknown.

Table of Contents

Appendix 2: YouTube Video Clips

Other Books

The following books are also available as hard copy or as e-books.

They contain lots of background material and specific Training Plans. You can find them any time by putting my name (Hertha James) into the Amazon search engine.

How to Begin Equine Clicker Training: Improve Horse-Human Communication

Conversations with Horses: An In-depth look at the Signals & Cues between Horses and their Handlers

Walking with Horses: The Eight Leading Positions

Learn Universal Horse Language: No Ropes

How to Create Good Horse Training Plans: The Art of Thin-Slicing

If you prefer e-books but don't have a Kindle reader, Amazon has a free Kindle reader which can be downloaded to any computer, tablet or smartphone.

The Author

Hertha James grew up in Calgary just east of the Rocky Mountains in Alberta, Canada. Her lifelong passion for horses began, age six, riding a big black horse. Animals of all kinds have always been an important part of her work and leisure.

Hertha's career with animals began with a zoology degree and includes working as a zookeeper in Calgary and Wellington, New Zealand, as well as handling wild and exotic species for movie parts. Her animal experiences stood her in good stead when she changed careers to become a high school teacher of science and biology.

Hertha's other passion, writing teaching and learning resources, grew from her experiences as a teacher.

Teaching science to teenagers for 23 years honed her ability to structure information clearly. It taught her how to build new knowledge in small steps and integrate it with the information and beliefs already held by her students.

Hertha applies the same successful strategy to teaching horses and their handlers. She shows that horse training goals can be reached when valid starting points are based on gentle experimentation followed by good planning.

Free YouTube Links Included

You can find my YouTube channel with a search for *Hertha Muddyhorse*. Please see Appendix 2 for a comprehensive list of titles. Relevant video clips are mentioned throughout the book.

These playlists mainly relate to the ideas in this book:

1. *HorseGym with Boots*: these are numbered. For example, if you would like to view Clip #18, simply put "*#18 HorseGym with Boots*" into the YouTube search engine and it should take you there. Each title starts with its number.

2. *Foot Care*: I've put the nine *HorseGym with Boots* clips, made specially to accompany this book (85-93 as listed below), into their own playlist, called *Foot Care*, so they are quicker to find.

   85. Foot care Prerequisites: Lead, Halt & Back-up
   86. Asking for One Step at a Time
   87. Stick Relaxation
   88. Foot Awareness
   89. Standing Square & Balance on Three Legs
   90. Asking for Each Foot with Touch Signals
   91. Asking for Each Foot from One Side
   92. The Hoof Stand and Hoof Sling
   93. Spray Bottle Confidence

3. *Free-Shaping*: These clips only have names. To find one, click on the playlist name and scroll down to find the title that you want.

4. *Thin-Slicing*: These clips also only have names so please scroll down the list to find the title you want to view.

Short Glossary

Behavior: that which is actually happening, not colored by our expectations or an emotional slant from our personal viewpoint.

Body Extensions: general name for the sticks, whips, wands, reeds, strings, ropes, halters, reins, bridles, saddles and harnesses that people use with horses.

Chaining: linking together a number of tasks where each one relates to the task that has gone before. For example, if we want to ride our horse with a saddle, we start with building confidence with a saddle pad. Then we might run a rope around the horse's girth so we can tighten and loosen it to simulate a girth. Then we introduce the saddle, first as an object to explore, then on the horse's back. When that is smooth, we add the girth, tightening it in easy stages while moving the horse between each new tightening. This chain would continue with teaching the horse to follow a target stick, standing relaxed at a mounting block, laying our weight across the horse, one foot in the stirrup, sitting on the horse, asking the horse to move by following a target stick or a person on the ground, and so on.

Click Point: the specific behavior that we are focusing on at the moment to enable the horse to earn a click&treat.

Clicker Training: general name for training using the 'mark and reward' system. We can use a mechanical clicker, a tongue click, a special word or any special sound to 'mark' the exact moment that the horse is doing what we want. The 'marker' sound is immediately followed by a small food treat. See Appendix 1 for more information about clicker training.

Click&treat: the 'click' marks the exact behavior we would like. The 'treat' follows immediately after the click. The horse will seek to repeat the behavior that produced the click followed by the treat. Clicker training is also called the 'mark and reward' system.

Comfort Zone: a general term for all the places where we feel at ease. All the activities we can do without anxiety fall into our comfort zone. There is more about comfort zones in Chapter 1.

Criteria: the expectations that we set for a specific lesson. For example, if we are teaching side-stepping facing a fence line, the expectation (criterion) for our first lesson may be to get one sideways step, at which point we click&treat. If that goes well, we may shift the expectation (criterion) for our next lesson to three sideways steps before we click&treat.

Emotional Neutrality: the ability to stay calm and not 'buy into' any upset that the horse or people around us are showing. Horses are highly tuned-in to the emotional state of other horses and people nearby. If we can remain calm, the horse is able to link in to our calmness. If we are nervous, afraid or fearful, the horse has no reason to feel comfortable with what we are asking him to do.

Free-shaping: using a *click&treat* to highlight any naturally occurring behavior we would like to 'capture' and make part of the horse's repertoire. For example, when we start clicker training by teaching the horse to touch his nose to a target object, we click&treat when the horse's natural curiosity causes him to touch his nose to our target.

We have 'captured' a behavior that was offered freely by the horse. We can then refine the behavior. We can ask the horse to move his head up, down, or to the side to touch the target.

We can ask him to move his feet to touch the target. Having the horse keen to seek out a target opens up a large range of training possibilities without the need for halters and ropes when we are in a safe, enclosed area.

Rather than putting pressure on the horse physically, we are setting him up with a puzzle and allowing him to solve it in his own time.

His motivation, rather than release of our signal pressure, is his instinctive seeking response to obtain more of what he likes (the treat that follows the click). There is more about this in Chapter 2.

Individual Education Program (IEP): anyone can write general Training Plans to teach something to a horse, but the horse's own handler has to refine a general Training Plan to suit the character type, age, health and background experience of the individual horse to be educated.

Additionally, the IEP considers all the same factors in relation to the handler. For example, although I was athletic in my youth, aged knees now set a limit to how fast and far I can move.

Inhibitors: anything we do and use to keep ourselves, our horse and others around us safe. Inhibitors can be fences, ropes and reins that keep the horse contained in a safe area. Inhibiting actions include the use of our arms and body extensions to block behaviors that may harm the horse, the handler or others.

Mark & Reward Training System: see 'Clicker Training'.

Negative reinforcement: removing signal pressure (which might be very light) or discomfort. Stopping an action the horse understands as a signal or stopping an action he finds bothersome.

Note, 'negative' is not used in the sense of being 'bad'. It is used in the mathematical sense of <u>subtracting</u> something (i.e. the signal pressure we have applied) from a situation. This is the most common type of reinforcement used by horse trainers.

Positive reinforcement: when the horse complies with a request, we highlight the moment with a marker signal and promptly deliver a treat. The treat has to be something the horse loves to receive, usually a tasty morsel.

Note that the term 'positive' is used in the mathematical sense of <u>adding</u> something to the situation, in this case a marker sound and a treat.

Many people think that the removal of their signal pressure is the 'reward' and therefore it is positive reinforcement. Actually, the release of the pressure is 'negative reinforcement' because the pressure has been removed.

This misunderstanding has led to a great deal of confusion for people trying to do their best with their horses.

Prerequisites: essential things the horse needs to know first, before we can expect him to confidently learn the new thing we want to teach him.

Reflex action: a term used for an instinctive response. It is something we or any animal does without thinking about it first. A reflex action can be to move 'away', like jerking our hand away when it touches something hot. Maybe our whole body jumps away when we see a cockroach in our sock drawer.

Generally, reflex actions are concerned with physical safety. One good jolt from an electric fence can modify our behavior around electric fences for a long time.

Horses, being prey animals, rely on flight for safety and have a strong set of instinctive responses. We need to be aware of these and recognize them for what they are: the natural reflex actions of a prey animal.

Release reinforcement: another name for 'negative reinforcement' – releasing (removing) pressure.

Reward reinforcement: another name for 'positive reinforcement' – adding the click&treat reward.

Shaping: when we want to teach something, we experiment to see what the horse can offer already. Then we carefully develop an IEP which allows us, using very small steps, to influence the horse's behavior until he can confidently carry out the total task we want to accomplish.

Signal pressure: whenever we show up and want the horse to do things with us, we are exerting signal pressure. The pressure can become an extremely light message of communication once the horse understands what we want. In some circumstances, the pressure will be more intense if we have to clarify a message or if safety is our first concern.

Thin-slicing: cutting a whole task into its smallest teachable (clickable) parts so we can teach the horse in a way that keeps him being continually successful.

Threshold: the point at which we begin to feel uneasy about a situation. Our breathing rate and heart rate increase, we sweat and may get funny feelings in our gut. The same things happen to horses when they reach threshold. Their confidence turns to anxiety. The better we are at realizing when horses reach threshold, the more effective our training will be. This is because we can ensure that the horse stays near or at threshold while he is learning, but we don't tip him over threshold, turning his responses into fear reactions. Once a horse or a person is over threshold, constructive learning is no longer possible because anxiety emotions have taken over.

Training Plan: an outline of the possible thin-slices that we might be able to use to teach horses a particular task. A Training Plan is the starting point for writing a specific Individual Education Program (IEP) that suits a specific handler, the specific horse and the specific training environments that they have available. (See also, Individual Education Program.)

Figure 1: Relaxed Foot Care: A good Training Plan customized into an Individual Education Program for a specific horse can make the teaching and learning process low-stress for the horse and the handler.

Chapter 1: Getting Ready

When we see that a horse needs foot care, it's only human to want to dive right in and try to get the hooves into better condition.

On the other hand, the feet are often the last thing about our horse that we feel comfortable about owning. Fortunately, there are now many books and online resources that make it easier to learn about the structure and function of horse feet, and how we can best look after them.

Before we delve into foot care, it pays to check that a few other things are in place first -- the prerequisites. Prerequisites are the behaviors the horse should have in his repertoire before we focus on foot care.

Figure 2: One prerequisite is that the horse leads willingly with a relaxed lead rope. Here Bridget and Boots are walking from mat to mat, with a tidy halt at each mat earning a click&treat.

Some horses may already be comfortable with most of the prerequisites. Other horses may have some or many of the prerequisites missing, making it important to carefully establish them first. Chapter 4 looks at the prerequisites in detail.

Foot care is a structured procedure with which any horse needs to be comfortable. By teaching the horse the structure that we plan to use, we make it easier for him to know what is going to happen before it happens. Like us, a horse can only relax if he knows, ahead of time, what is about to happen.

The structure that I suggest in this book should not limit anyone's own creativity to design ways of doing things that best suit themselves and their horse.

My structure is not a formula but it can become a checklist of the essential elements that help lead to stress-free foot care. By initially having a structure to follow, it's easier to master the concept and craft. In other words:

- learn the structure

- follow the structure and get the feel of it

- change the structure to suit your own situation.

I use reward reinforcement in all my training. Reward reinforcement is usually called equine clicker training. The ideas in this book are based on clicker training.

If you are not already an equine clicker trainer, please see Appendix 1 for a set of notes about how to get started. To stay hands-free, most horse clicker trainers use a tongue click or a special sound or word instead of a mechanical clicker.

It works just fine to use a marker word like 'yes' or 'good' (and try not to use the words otherwise) but it's best to use a made-up word or sound. I've used 'ubu' and 'biff' in the past with good success. A made-up word is less likely to show up in our speech, so it will be easier for the horse to fix a meaning to it. A word in a second language is another possibility.

The marker word or sound is the key to training with reward reinforcement. The moment the horse does what we want, we sound the marker and follow it up promptly with a very small food treat. I use small carrot strips or pony pellets. Other options are given in Appendix 1.

Reward reinforcement allows us to use free-shaping (see glossary) to develop the behavior we want, as well as guided shaping. For guided shaping, we use touch and gesture to help the horse understand what we want. When we use touch and gesture, the marker signal is usually simultaneous with the release of the touch or gesture pressure, so the horse has three sources of information that he has done the 'right thing' in our eyes.

1. The signal pressure is released.

2. He hears the marker sound.

3. A desired treat is promptly delivered.

In other words, for guided shaping, we use release reinforcement and reward reinforcement together to create clarity for the horse. Clicker-savvy horses tend to search actively for the answer we want, so our touch or gesture pressure seldom needs to be very strong.

Part A: Are the Handler & Horse Clicker-Savvy?

Figure 3: Bridget is delivering a treat after a click for Boots' willing halt on the tarp.

If you are an experienced equine clicker trainer, you can dive right into working through the outlines and tweaking them to suit you and your equines.

If you started equine clicker training recently, have a look at Appendix 1 to see if it all sounds familiar.

If you are new to reward reinforcement (clicker training), Appendix 1 has the information you need to get started. For more detailed information, see my book, *How to Begin Equine Clicker Training.*

Part B: Working with the Fear Factor

Many people are nervous about picking up a horse's feet. It helps to remember that our anxiety is tiny compared to the fear a horse experiences if he has not been introduced to foot care with thought to his feelings.

Horses know that if their feet are compromised, their number might be up. A wild horse that can't run knows he is on the menu for the next predator to come along. His feet are his only defense. Predators commonly dodge in and hamstring the prey animal, then follow it until it is weak and slow enough to make the kill.

We know ourselves how helpless we feel if we twist an ankle break a leg or are hobbled by knee pain.

Likewise, it's perfectly natural for us to feel fear about approaching the feet of a horse we don't know well. We don't know what will happen. We fear the unknown and we are fearful because we know that we can get hurt if we get it wrong. Then who would look after our horse?

It's vitally important that we recognize and acknowledge our own fear thresholds and deal with ourselves in the same thoughtful and constructive way that we will deal with our horse.

When it comes to asking a horse to surrender a foot to our 'care', it pays to teach the skill carefully and thoroughly, and not leave it to other people such as farriers or barefoot trimmers.

Move Closer, Stay Longer

The title above is from a book by Stephanie Burns. It is a book full of the fears Stephanie faced, and the strategies she developed to overcome them, as she learned about horses. Working with Pat and Linda Parelli, she took on the challenge of learning to care for and ride a horse, starting as a total (and freaked out) beginner. Details of the book are in the Reference List. If you can find a copy, it is a worthwhile read.

To build our confidence around handling a horse's feet, we must begin at the point just before our confidence slips into anxiety. It is my hope that the structure I've presented here can work equally well to build the confidence of:

- a horse who is new to, or wary about, foot handling

- a person who is new to, or wary about, handling a horse's feet.

Ideal 1: If you are nervous, can you find a 'been there, done that' horse with whom you can build your handling skills and competence?

Ideal 2: You are already confident around horses but want some ideas about how to make foot care easier for a horse who comes with unwanted foot care baggage or is new to foot care.

Not so Ideal: A nervous handler together with an anxious horse is not the best, but with time and care, progress will be made. It might take a bit longer, depending on how often you can do short sessions.

It helps if the handler can stay in his or her *comfort zone* when asking more of the horse. It helps if the horse can be relaxed in a familiar place when the handler works on his own anxiety.

The ultimate aim is to have foot care be a relaxed, every day, ho-hum experience without the need for tranquilizers for the participants on either end of the lead rope.

The following section about Comfort Zones is borrowed from my book, *How to Create Good Horse Training Plans*.

Comfort Zones

When we begin to do new things, it takes time and effort to get the feel of what we are doing. Getting this 'feel' for a new activity doesn't happen in ten minutes.

Doing something new takes us out of our comfort zone. We know when we are out of our comfort zone because our heart rate and breathing speed up. We may sweat more and have feelings of un-ease, often beginning in our gut or stomach.

It's important to recognize how we feel when we are out of our comfort zone, as well as how we feel when we are back in our comfort zone.

Only desire, effort and application can make our comfort zone larger. Learning and education are all about expanding comfort zones.

Obviously, both the handler and the horse have comfort zones. If both parties are out of their comfort zones, it may not be a good horse day. So, it's important that when the handler is out of his or her comfort zone, the horse is in his comfort zone.

When we take the horse out of his comfort zone, we ideally want to remain in our own comfort zone so we can maintain our emotional neutrality. By understanding our own and our horse's comfort zones, we'll have more good horse days until every day is a good horse day.

At times a horse may find 'comfort' if he is given freedom to move and run, using up adrenalin and enlarging his personal space.

At another time the same horse may find 'comfort' in a quiet, restful state.

As the handler gets a better understanding of the edges of a horse's comfort zones, it becomes easier and easier to thin-slice tasks to suit that particular horse.

The following diagram has six arrows that illustrate the six situations that a person or horse will come across.

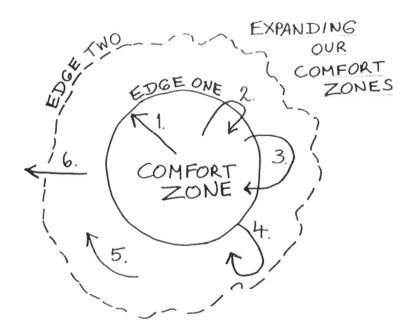

Figure 4: Comfort Zones: All of us, horse or human, have a 'comfort zone' within which our heart rate is normal and we can allow ourselves to relax. Expanding a comfort zone takes active intent. The six numbers are explained shortly.

The inner circle with the smooth boundary is the existing comfort zone. We can call this boundary **Edge One** because it is a threshold that determines our behavior.

To expand our comfort zone, we have to move out toward the broken line. Out there is the world with all kinds of thresholds. We can call the broken line **Edge Two**.

The numbers with the arrows on the diagram refer to the six situations that will arise whenever a person or a horse is faced with expanding their comfort zone:

1. Lacking confidence to leave the comfort zone.

2. Can leave the comfort zone for a bit, but then has to hurry back.

3. Able to leave the comfort zone for longer before going back.

4. No longer needs to retreat to the former comfort zone. The comfort zone has expanded.

5. Starting to feel comfortable well beyond the old **Edge One** threshold.

6. I can do this now. What is the next challenge? I'm ready to set a new **Edge Two**. **Edge One** has moved out to encompass the original **Edge Two**. The comfort zone has expanded.

If we push ourselves, or the horse, toward **Edge Two** too quickly or too soon, we, or the horse, will feel worried, anxious or fearful.

We will 'run away' in our mind and make up reasons to avoid going 'out there' again. The horse will indicate that he'd like to leave the situation or he will 'shut down'. Either one means he has given up trying to understand what we'd like him to do.

This avoidance response is the brain's way of keeping us safe. It's a useful instinct in some situations, but in today's world, and with horses forced to live in captivity, we have to find ways of successfully expanding our comfort zones.

As we learn to recognize where we and the horse are in relation to our comfort zones for any given situation, we will be able to take more control of where we are, in relation to where we want to be.

Safety is always the first priority. The horse has to learn how to respond appropriately to a variety of human pressures. The handler must know how to influence the horse to keep everyone safe when a stressful situation occurs.

A stressful situation can arise in a split second. It helps a great deal if the horse has faith in us and if we know how the horse will probably respond to a strong signal we may have to use when his adrenalin is up.

The suggestions outlined in this book are designed to help you reach your objective (calm, confident, enjoyable foot care) by helping you determine your current comfort zones.

Then the exercises are designed to move you and your horse beyond your current comfort zones, but not too fast. Good horse training generally has the appearance of paint drying. The best training keeps the handler and the horse being successful so that progress appears seamless. We don't have to raise the dust.

Part C: Outline of a Foot Care Plan

We'll begin with an overall summary of the Planning Process itself, illustrated with foot care particulars. This summary is taken from the end of my book, *How to Create Good Horse Training Plans*.

1. Decide on the Topics

Everything we do with our horse should be designed to increase his confidence in the human-dominated world he lives in. If we are watching and listening, the horse usually tells us what we should work on next.

Our topic is foot care, but if some basic prerequisite skills are missing, we may have to first work with:

- haltering
- leading
- everyday care procedures
- rope relaxation and calmness
- relaxation while tied up
- staying parked unsecured at a target, or ground-tied.

Each of the above topics includes a series of related tasks.

2. Scope the Topic & Seek the Prerequisites

If our purpose is to pick up the horse's feet to clean them or get them trimmed, and we are not rich in knowledge about the sensitivity and nature of horses, we may head straight for a foot and see how it goes.

However, if we want to influence the behavior of a horse (or any animal, child or other person) in a positive way, it is important to find the right starting point. The right starting point is where the student feels comfortable.

If a horse is anxious about haltering, leads erratically, barges through gates and turns his butt to you when you arrive with his hay or hard feed, then planning specifically for foot care is a bit further down the road while we deal with haltering, leading, gate safety and safety around food.

In other words, we seek out the prerequisites that need to be in place before we create a training plan focused only on foot care.

Prerequisites:

Our final goal (calm, confident foot care) is a complex series of behaviors. We achieve our goal by teaching a set of related tasks that are gradually chained together.

Foot care might look like a simple task at first glance. But a whole series of prerequisite mini-skills need to be in place so we have a solid foundation on which the new task can be built.

We can't expect a horse to stand still willingly, while we do things to him, unless we have quietly and carefully taught him that standing still without being tied up is okay. *#20 HorseGym with Boots* looks at *The Art of Standing Still.*

We can't expect a horse to be okay with us picking up his left front foot unless we have gone through a careful program of confidence-building designed for that specific horse.

Scoping your topic on paper goes hand in hand with mild experimentation with the horse to get a good idea of what the two of you can do already. Once you've experimented a bit, it's easier to decide what your first task should be.

3. Define Specific Tasks

When you have decided on your first topic, it's time to pick one aspect that you want to use as a first task to teach the horse. We can outline the decreasing complexity of what we are teaching like this:

Topic: relaxed daily care routines including foot care

    Goal: calm, confident, enjoyable foot care

        Tasks: (x4) each foot can be handled easily

            Thin-slices: for achieving each task; these create the custom-made plan for your horse (which may vary with each foot).

Thin-slices allow us to achieve a task. Several tasks allow us to achieve a goal. The goal is part of a larger training topic.

It's important to set tasks that you can achieve in a relatively short time frame. You may have a horse that easily transfers teaching about one foot to the other three feet. Or you may have a horse, due to reasons we will never know, who has a different emotional response for each foot.

It may take months to achieve our major goal. But the tasks leading to that goal should be small enough so that the horse and the handler continuously experience small successes.

Foot care is a special task because it has four sub-tasks. We start again, at the beginning of our teaching plan, with each foot. Front feet present a different challenge to back feet.

If we are right handed, working on the horse's left side may be easier for us. Vice versa if we are left handed. Similarly, horses have a preferred side. Natural asymmetry of a horse's body can cause different imbalances when we ask him to stand on three legs.

Defining a task is made easier by using a structure called the **ABCD** method because it forces us to be specific. When you outline a task with the **ABCD** structure (detailed below), your Training Plan can progress nicely. It will be easy to adjust the plan as you get feedback from yourself and the horse. Not defining a task clearly is a major hurdle to good planning and good training outcomes.

ABCD Method

A = **Audience**: think of the horse's character type and what best motivates him. What do you think he may find easy or hard? If you are coaching another person, consider the character type of the person too. If you are working by yourself, consider your own character type. We'll look at this in a bit more detail later.

B = **Behavior**: exactly what do you want to see when the horse is carrying out the task the way you want? When we are handling feet, it is easy to feel the horse's tension or relaxation. Additionally, how do you want your signals for the horse to look and feel? What will your signals actually be (how will you be behaving to tell the horse what you want)?

C = **Conditions**: in what venue, with what props, in what environment, with or without head gear, rope? The safest horse is a horse at liberty. A horse who is free to leave a situation is a horse who can learn at his own pace. I started trimming my own horses' feet in 2004. After I took up clicker training in 2008 the horses learned to stay parked on a mat unrestrained, making it all much easier.

D = **Degree of Perfection or Proficiency**: how are you going to measure what you are doing? With foot care, we want to end up with a reasonably high level of proficiency. When we ask for the foot, we need it up long enough to clean or trim, although we can give the foot back whenever the horse asks for it, then resume. Once you have taught the basic task of lifting the foot, you can gradually build duration.

As well as foot care for cleaning and inspection, how proficient do you want your horse to be with another person handling his feet for trimming?

4. Venues, Props and Time

Write down possible training venues, time at your disposal, time it may take the horse to learn the task plus the props and helpers you have available.

You outlined the **conditions** for teaching when you defined your task. Now is the time to work out the detail of where and when and how you can ensure the conditions that will make the teaching and learning as easy as possible.

This is especially important if you must work around other people at a boarding facility.

5. Brainstorm Possible Thin-Slices

All your thinking about your defined task is now put to work to create a brainstorm or mind map of the smallest parts (slices) that make up the overall task.

Remember, it's easy to have too few slices, but we can never have too many. The more we can keep the horse feeling successful, the more he will enjoy his sessions.

Using mind maps as part of our planning make it easy to think about and visualize the slices and decide the most logical order for tackling them.

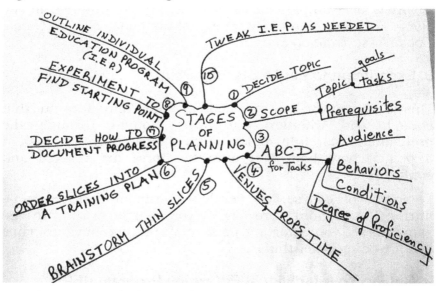

Figure 5: A mind map of ten steps we can use to plan an Individual Education Program for a specific horse.

6. Thin-Slices in Order = Training Plan

Once you have brainstormed a list, or a mind map, of the smallest slices you can think of, it's time to put them into an order that might work nicely for you and the horse.

As always, you can add, delete or move your ideas around. If you've thought through the slices on paper, it's easier to work with them when you're out with the horse. Pocket cue cards with the slices listed in order can be helpful. I generally use these if I'm working on a complex task.

When you've completed this step, your Training Plan is done!

7. Decide How You Will Document Your Progress

Before you move from your Training Plan into your Individual Education Program, decide how you will keep a record of what you're doing, when you did it and how it went during each session.

A variety of examples for record-keeping are outlined in the *Horse Folder* section of Chapter 4 of my book, *How to Create Good Horse Training Plans*.

8. Experiment to Find a Starting Point

This is where you find out whether your thin-slices are thin enough and whether you have thought through the prerequisites carefully enough. You want to begin the task at a point where both you and the horse are relaxed and confident.

You can, of course, do gentle experimentation any time during the planning process. If you mostly work with the same horse, your starting point may become obvious while you are doing other things.

9. Outline Your Individual Education Program (IEP)

Now is the time to customize your Training Plan by considering the character type, health, age, fitness level and background experience of your horse and yourself. You already considered this to some extent when you thought about the **A**udience portion of the **ABCD** structure, if you used that to define your task.

Your experimentation may show that your Training Plan was too ambitious and you need to slow down and do more thin-slicing of certain parts or add in tasks that need improvement. Or you may discover that the horse knows more than you realized, so you can drop some of the foundation lessons from the IEP.

You may discover that your horse finds something extra difficult, so you give that more time and attention. Life, weather or injury may interfere, forcing you to adjust the time frame.

You may decide your defined task was too large, so you go back to redefine it until it feels like a task you can master in a shorter time frame. As mentioned earlier, it's important that the tasks you set are achievable in a relatively short time. Each small success is worth its weight in gold for motivation to keep learning.

10. Tweak Your IEP

Each session with your horse gives you valuable feedback and new ideas. Things that *don't* work are just as valuable as things that *do* work. By using a pre-planned set of thin-slices, we can avoid a lot of unfocused activity that confuses the horse and leads to handler frustration.

Inevitably, we'll still get occasional confusion. The IEP is always a work in progress. Tweak it as you get new information by listening to your horse and when you make new connections as you think through a challenge.

Part D: About Horse Feet

More and more people are realizing that attaching live, dynamic tissue to inflexible steel horseshoes causes most of the lameness problems that arise with domestic horses. A well-maintained natural foot, realistic feeding regime paired with as much movement over 24 hours as possible, all contribute to healthy feet.

The Internet is a wonderful resource to find out more about barefoot trimming. Books and hands-on clinics are available in many places. It's not hard to learn, and many people now enjoy looking after their own horses' feet.

The horse foot is designed to be rugged. It expands as the foot hits the ground heel first. Much of the impact is absorbed by the frog, the solar cushion in the back of the foot, and the natural flexion of the sole. After impact, the foot rolls forward onto the toes. These actions act like an extra pump to help send blood from the foot back up the long leg to the heart.

Horse feet are designed to accommodate a great deal of movement every day. Such movement was necessary in the sparse grassland habitats where horses evolved. During much of the year extensive movement was needed to find enough fodder and to access water. So, extensive, low impact movement (walking) is a cornerstone of healthy feet.

It is easy to see why horses kept stabled or yarded for much of their lives will have poor foot circulation. Sluggish circulation means oxygen arrives less often. Waste products are not removed promptly, compromising all the bones, connective tissue ligaments and tendons in the foot.

If we add steel shoes to the equation, circulation is compromised even more because the shod foot cannot expand and contract in the way it is designed to do.

The tendons and ligaments of the lower leg have very little protection. Adding a steel shoe adds a centrifugal force to the leg every time the horse takes a step, putting extra strain on the tendons and ligaments.

A barefoot horse can feel a great deal through his feet. He will place his feet with more care and therefore be much more sure-footed.

It takes at least six weeks to transition a shod horse to barefoot if we can walk the horse daily for a mile or so on pavement. My current horse, now 14, has never been shod. I had good success transitioning an elderly Thoroughbred. Her feet turned into gravel-crunchers.

Beyond the trauma of shoes on a shod horse, the state of a horse's feet depends on several factors such as:

- inherited characteristics
- diet, historical and present
- amount of daily movement
- type of surfaces the horse lives on
- nature of the foot care received.

A good barefoot trim has special features that are outlined in the many resources available. Some of these resources are listed in the Reference Section.

Chapter 2: Goal and Conditions

The **ABCD** structure for setting behavioral objectives is handy, but we don't have to use it in the **ABCD** order. We will start with **D**, which stands for **D**egree of Proficiency. In other words, how well do we want the task to be carried out before we feel that we have finished teaching it?

At what point will relaxed foot care become an everyday habit and routine?

Once we've decided the **D**egree of Proficiency, we can outline **C**, the **C**onditions under which we expect the horse to be able to achieve our goal.

Degree of Proficiency for our Foot Care Goal

The final behavior we would like to establish is that the horse lifts each foot confidently, on request, to allow cleaning, inspection and trimming.

This goal looks so short and concise. Who would think there are a multitude of mini-skills needed to achieve it in a relaxed manner?

Figure 6: Boots is learning to balance comfortably on three legs by targeting her knee to Bridget's hand. It's one of Boots' favorite clicker games. We play it daily.

Conditions for the Horse

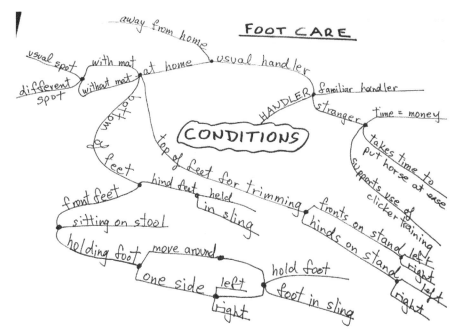

Figure 7: A mind map outlining conditions to consider.

In most circumstances, we look after the horse's feet when he is at his home in a space where he feels confident and can relax.

We first need him to be comfortable with his usual handler, but once that is established, we may want to expand the horse's comfort zone to include one or more other people.

Handler position needs consideration. You may prefer to move around the horse as you do each foot. I like to clean all the feet from the horse's left side, since I am right-handed. If you are left-handed, you may prefer to do them all from the left side. Staying on one side saves time and I find it easier on my back.

For trimming, I may sit on a stool to trim the bottom of the front feet, resting the foot on my knee. Alternatively, I may use a hoof-jack with a sling and ask the horse to rest his foot in the sling.

Figure 8: If we want to use a sling on a hoof-jack, we have another skill to carefully teach the horse.

When we are teaching *foot care confidence*, each of these differences are highly meaningful to the horse. We need to teach each variation by thin-slicing it carefully.

For foot trimming, he also has to know how to put his foot forward and up onto a hoof-stand.

Figure 9: We can build duration of the front foot on a hoof stand by gradually withholding the click&treat a tiny bit longer. I like to go up in one second increments.

If we take our horse out and about, either walking or riding, he may pick up a stone or have a foot injury, so it is good to generalize confidence about picking up feet in situations away from home.

We may ask a farrier or barefoot trimmer to work on his feet. His feet may need checking by a vet. These are conditions we can simulate to generalize the skills before a foot care event is imminent. Whenever the opportunity arises, have a new person ask your horse for his feet.

For each variation in the conditions, it is up to us to create a custom-designed Individual Education Plan suited to the individual horse. We want the tasks thin-sliced finely enough so that the horse can be continually successful with his learning.

To review the idea of thin-slicing, here is a summary taken from my book, *Conversations with Horses*.

Thin-Slicing Explained

When we observe someone else's horse perform a finished behavior, it is often tempting to try it ourselves with our horse, by repeating it as we saw it. But that is **not** how it works.

When we want to train something new, the first step is to experiment a bit to see what the horse can offer already, in relation to the new goal we'd like to achieve. This will give us an idea of where our Individual Education Program (IEP) needs to start. We want to base it on foundation training with which the horse is already confident.

It is also a good way to find any 'training holes' that we need to fill before we enthusiastically head toward setting a new challenge for the horse.

Once we have a starting point, we can begin to write our IEP by thin-slicing the overall task.

The first step of thin-slicing is a brainstorm to dissect the complete task into its smallest teachable components. Then we have to organize these components or 'slices' into an order that we think will make sense to our horse. This possible order of slices becomes the basis of our IEP. What makes sense to any particular horse will depend on:

- his innate character type
- his previous life experiences
- the degree of communication that already exists between the horse and the handler
- frequency of the training sessions
- how comfortable the horse feels in the training environment
- effective, creative use of objects and obstacles to make it easier for the horse to understand our intent.

An IEP is always a 'work in progress' and usually we go back and tweak it many times. Sometimes we throw the whole thing out and start again. Each time we work with the horse, we get additional feedback from the horse and from our own reactions and responses.

Thin-slicing means carefully checking (and re-checking) that the horse is comfortable and confident with each tiny slice of the process before we move on. It pays to remember that the *process* of teaching does not look like the finished product.

We need to balance the need to build confidence at each tiny step with the need to move on when we should, so the horse doesn't get bored. It's never easy to walk the fine line between moving too fast and going too slowly.

It all becomes easier as experience:

- gives us a deeper understanding of a particular horse's character type
- improves our reading of the nuances of horse body language
- makes us more aware of our own body language and the messages we are giving
- improves our thin-slicing, so creating better Individual Education Programs.

Successive Approximations

In simple English, this means that we start with what the horse can offer already and gradually direct and reward each tiny change in the direction of the final behavior we want.

In other words, at the beginning of teaching something new, we release (click&treat) for the slightest approximation of what we want as our final result. Each approximation becomes one slice of the overall task.

Each time the horse feels ready, we encourage him to do a tiny bit more to gain the release (click&treat). This whole process of rewarding successive approximations is called 'shaping' a behavior.

A human example of 'shaping a behavior' is teaching a child to write. We start with holding a pencil and using it to make random marks on paper. At some point the random marks become conscious curves and straight lines.

When the time is right, we introduce writing the letters of the alphabet. Eventually the child can group letters to make words. Words are then arranged into meaningful sentences. Some children go on to write coherent paragraphs, essays, stories or books.

If the child loses confidence with any of the 'slices' of the process, an element of discomfort can creep in, along with typical avoidance behavior. Not enough practice then results in a poorly shaped skill.

Writing is an interesting human endeavour that starts at two years old and is still in formative stages ten years later.

Another way to look at successive approximations is to think of a sculptor starting with a piece of stone. He works in careful stages until the shape in his mind is visible to the rest of us in the shape of the sculpture.

In the same way, we gradually tease a series of movements (or stillness) out of a horse to yield a complete task. This is a bit harder than shaping stone because horses have minds of their own.

Chapter 3: Audience

In the **ABCD** structure for writing behavioral objectives, **A** stands for **A**udience. The process of defining our **A**udience is the same whether we are holding a seminar for many people or designing a program for one horse.

We define our horse by contemplating:

- his character type
- his age
- his physical health
- his mental health
- his living conditions
- his history as far as we can know it
- the sort of training techniques to which he has been exposed
- his understanding of how to get along with people
- his understanding of basic skills such as haltering, leading, tying up, transport, grooming
- his confidence with things like vet inspection, dental care, inoculations, worming
- his responses to saddling and riding or harnessing and driving, if these are part of his life.

Horse Character Types

There is much more information about character type in my book, *How to Create Good Horse Training Plans*.

Basically, horses tend to fall into two categories: those who move their feet easily and those who do not.

A horse may **move his feet easily** for one of two main reasons:

1. The horse is a bold, high-energy exuberant type of character who enjoys movement. If he feels bored, he will make his own excitement. This is a fun type of horse for handlers who are confident and can engage the horse in activities that he enjoys. Such horses are often described as spirited.

2. The horse has a high fear threshold and needs to move his feet due to anxiety when he does not understand a situation. Such horses are often described as flighty. This type of horse does best with a handler who is empathetic with the horse's comfort zones. With kind, consistent handling by a trusted person, at a pace set by the horse, this type of horse can become bolder. They can develop into athletic and willing companions.

A horse may **be reluctant to move his feet** for one of two main reasons.

1. The horse has an energy-conserving character by nature. He is generally bold and fairly laid back unless something significant activates his adrenalin. Such horses are often described as lazy or stubborn. They are usually highly food-motivated and thrive with reward reinforcement in the form of clicker training. They do best with a person who motivates them in novel ways and who values their reliability once they learn a task.

2. The horse has an anxious nature and tends to freeze. In the wild, this type of horse would probably tend to move his feet like the high-fear-threshold horse described above. In captivity, these horses seem to internalize their fear, causing them to freeze rather than move. Restriction by ropes and small pens have created enough trauma to make these horses give up their own ideas and 'shut down'. Such horses may be described as quiet. This sort of horse does best with a handler who is willing to slow down and wait for the horse to offer behaviors that can be rewarded. With a

handler willing to put in the time to earn the horse's trust, these horses can blossom into expressing their true personalities.

Any good teacher carefully considers the nature of their **A**udience when designing the presentation they want to give. The more aware we are about the nature of our horse, the more accurately we can design a suitable Individual Education Program.

If we are working with our own horse, rather than coaching another horse-person partnership, it is valuable to look at the way we tend to do things.

Our approach has much to do with the results we achieve. If we tend to become anxious and reactive around our horse, it's possible to learn ways of relaxing and how to foster emotional neutrality.

Most people have fond memories of some teachers and less-fond memories of others. Horses are the same. When we open our minds to explore different ways of being with our horse, we'll notice differences in the way the horse responds toward us.

Emotional Neutrality

This short piece is borrowed from my book, *How to Create Good Horse Training Plans*.

What makes sense to the horse will also depend on how we present each new slice of the task. The handler's personality and teaching approach is hugely significant. The horse is obviously also influenced by the following factors.

1. The horse immediately picks up the handler's emotional state. Horses are comfortable with emotional neutrality but seem to thrive with cheerfulness.

2. If the handler has good control of his or her energy levels, energy level becomes a meaningful signal and the horse can learn to match his energy to that of the handler, either in movement or in relaxation.

3. If the handler can temporarily set aside life's tensions and engage with mindfulness of the horse's more timeless approach to life, dwelling in the moment rather than the past or the future, it's possible for the horse to relax in the handler's company.

4. When an exercise goes awry, if the handler can 'pretend' it went well, remove pressure, smile, count to ten and reset the exercise, the horse is not made to feel wrong. The horse is then usually willing to try again. This sort of 'pretending' might seem bizarre at first, but it allows us to smile and the horse to relax. It strongly counterbalances our natural tendency to get tense and frustrated. It is a learned response we can build into our training technique.

The short section below called Patience Technique is borrowed from my book, *Walking with Horses*.

Patience Technique

It's helpful to teach ourselves a patience technique. This can be a struggle at first. It may require quite a mental shift in how we perceive our horse and what we are asking him to do.

Patience techniques can include some or all the responses listed below. As soon as we feel the first hint of frustration, we can do things like:

- consciously take several deep breaths

- turning our energy off; maybe turn away from the horse

- rolling our shoulders to relax them

- taking up a neutral body stance that will become our default position whenever we feel frustration starting up or need to give the horse time to return to relaxation

Figure 10: Bridget demonstrates the neutral body stance we use when we are not asking for anything from the horse. Both hands folded across the belly button is our signal for Boots that we are 'at ease'. Bridget's focus is away from the horse.

- remembering that we have taken the horse out of his normal herd life and expect him to put up with things a horse living naturally would never come across

- smiling as we realize we've just done the right thing by defusing our tension or frustration rather than letting it influence our actions

- counting numbers until the frustration fades away

- sitting down for a while or taking the horse to a grazing spot

- deciding to quietly finish the session.

First, we become mindful that we can lower our frustration rate by doing things like these. Eventually we may remember to apply them more and more when we are out with the horse.

A relationship with a horse is a two-way fusion between the character of the horse and the character of the handler. Success will flow when the handler can appreciate the character type of the horse, and adjust his or her behavior to draw from the horse the best that the horse can give at the time.

Many horses are trapped as playthings to pander to the ego of people who want to win competitions. Unfortunately, most horse sports are not sporting for the horses.

Chapter 4: Prerequisite Behaviors

When we use the **ABCD** structure to write behavioral objectives to help achieve our goal, the **B** stands for the specific **B**ehaviors that we want to develop into habits that will make our life easier and the horse's life easier.

To create a habit, we teach carefully using a process that keeps the horse being successful as much as possible. Success builds on success.

We want each slice of teaching secure in the horse's deep memory. Deep memory is formed with repeated, relaxed short sessions to develop a skill. Each quiet repeat strengthens the nerve pathway. Some things will be learned quickly. Other things may take much longer than expected.

We chain the successive slices together until eventually the horse can carry out the whole task with one reward at the end. When Boots and I do daily foot cleaning, I click&treat for standing squarely. Then I click&treat for the lifting of the left front foot. It's easy to get the treat out of my pocket and give to her while I hold the foot. After that, I ask for 'foot up' with a touch signal on each leg as I get to it. When all four are done, there is a final click&treat.

Figure 11: We have a routine where we click&treat for the front left leg lifted and another click&treat after cleaning all four feet.

When I began thinking about the whole topic of foot care, it became clear that many tasks contribute to a horse's ability to be relaxed and confident about yielding his feet to us.

Our topic is foot care. But before we head into picking up the horse's feet, we want to take a hard look at the prerequisites needed to make the horse relatively comfortable with the idea of surrendering his foot to us.

Here are some questions we should ask.

1. Is the handler clicker-savvy? In other words, does he or she already use reward reinforcement (clicker training) smoothly for teaching this horse?

2. Is the horse clicker-savvy? Does he understand that what he was doing when he heard the click is what will earn him a treat, so he willingly repeats that action (or inaction if we want him to stand still)?

Figure 12: If we are clicker-savvy, we know that we must click at the moment the leg is <u>lifting</u>, so the horse understands that it is the 'lift' that we want.

3. Does the horse willingly walk on, halt and back up with light signals?

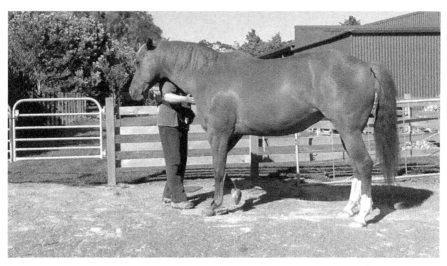

Figure 13: Boots willingly backs up with a light touch signal at her chest. This will be useful later when I ask her to stand squarely or back a foot off a hoof stand.

4. Are you able to ask the horse to move one step at a time, forward or back?

5. Have you played lots of games asking the horse to place his feet accurately on things like mats, pedestals, beam balance or in hoops? Has the horse learned to pop balloons with a foot and place individual feet over a rail? In other words, have you done fun exercises that encourage the horse to be 'foot aware'?

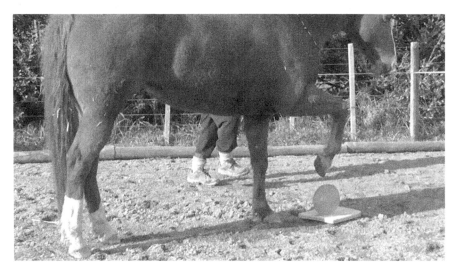

Figure 14: Popping balloons is a great exercise for helping the horse become more 'foot aware'.

Figure 15: Bridget is asking Boots to put her front feet on the beam balance. She models the 'step up' and Boots follows.

Figure 16. Learning to stand on a beam balance with all four feet is an excellent way to encourage a horse to become more aware of positioning his feet.

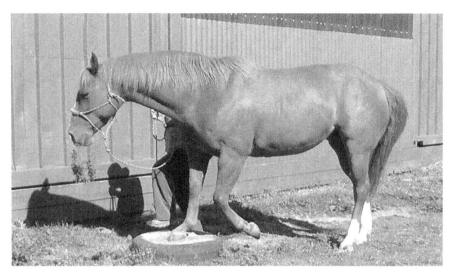

Figure 17: A tire filled with rocks and soil makes a secure, safe pedestal for teaching the acts of stepping up and stepping down on request, encouraging foot awareness.

Figure 18: A stump can be handy to prepare the horse for bringing each front foot forward onto a hoof stand.

Figure 19: Boots is carefully stepping both hind feet out of the hoop while keeping her front feet in the other hoop.

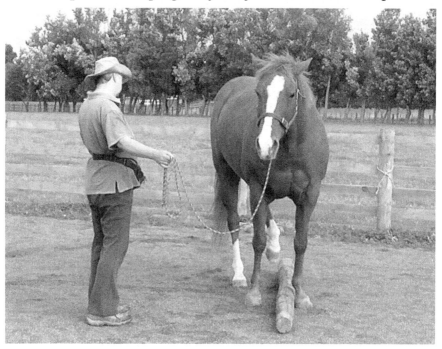

Figure 20: Learning to straddle a rail helps foot awareness.

6. Does the horse readily target a mat with his front feet?

7. Does the horse easily stand on a large mat or tarp with all four feet?

8. Can the horse stand still in a relaxed manner (stay parked) for a minute or longer?

Figure 21: Learning to stand relaxed on a mat in our usual foot care spot helps to build confidence because it lets the horse know that it is time for foot care. Horses like to know what is going to happen before it happens, just as we do.

9. Do you have a designated spot for foot care where the horse can relax and others can't interfere?

10. Is the horse comfortable about having a whip, stick or pool noodle rubbed all over his body, including up and down the legs?

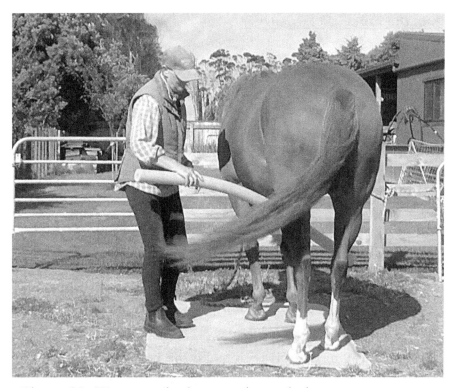

Figure 22: We want the horse to be cool about an assortment of body extensions rubbed all over his body.

If the answer is yes to the above ten questions, we can delve into the actual foot care procedures.

If the answer is no for some or all of them, these questions need to be addressed before heading into foot care procedures.

Background Information Available

My other books, and their accompanying video clips, have lots of information about some of the prerequisite tasks, as outlined below.

1. Is the handler clicker-savvy?

If you don't already use clicker training, Appendix 1 gives you enough information to get started. More detail is in my book, *How to Begin Equine Clicker Training*.

2. Is the horse clicker-savvy?

As 1 above.

3. Does the horse walk on, halt & back up with light signals?

This is covered in detail:

- in my book, *Walking with Horses*
- clips *#27-#30 HorseGym with Boots* (inclusive)
- in *#39-#40 HorseGym with Boots,* which illustrate the main ideas
- in *#85 HorseGym with Boots.*

4. Can you ask the horse to move one step at a time?

One step at a time is detailed in:

- Training Plan 6 in section 33-10 of my book, *Conversations with Horses.*
- *#86 HorseGym with Boots.*

5. Have you done exercises to make the horse 'foot aware'?

Teaching about mats, rails, stumps, pedestals, beam balances, targeting with knees and hocks -- all designed to create foot awareness -- are found:

- as Training Plan Four in my book, *How to Begin Equine Clicker Training*
- in clips *#6-#12 HorseGym with Boots* (inclusive)
- *in clips #14, #15, #18, #20, #22* and *#24 HorseGym with Boots* which illustrate many of the concepts
- in a series of five clips about stepping into and out of hoops in my playlist called *Hula Hoop Challenges.*
- in *#88 HorseGym with Boots* which illustrates some foot awareness tasks
- in *#89 HorseGym with Boots* which looks at square halts and standing on three legs by targeting with knees and hocks.

6. Does the horse readily target a mat with his front feet?

As 5 above.

7. Does the horse stand on a large mat with all four feet?

As 5 above.

8. Can the horse stand relaxed for a minute or longer?

As 5 above and specifically

- *#8 HorseGym with Boots.*

9. Is the horse relaxed being rubbed with body extensions?

- *#87 HorseGym with Boots*

10. Do you have a designated spot for foot care?

Decide on a good spot for foot care and use it consistently. Once the horse is comfortable standing on a mat with duration, we can use the mat as the 'spot' and vary where we put it.

Figure 23: Once our horse loves mats because they are a place of ample reward reinforcement, we can set up 'a place to park' with just a small mat.

Chapter 5: Front Foot Behaviors

If the horse and handler have a relaxed relationship that includes clicker training as well as smooth 'walk on', 'halt', 'back up' and 'please stay parked here', it's time to look at tasks specific to foot care.

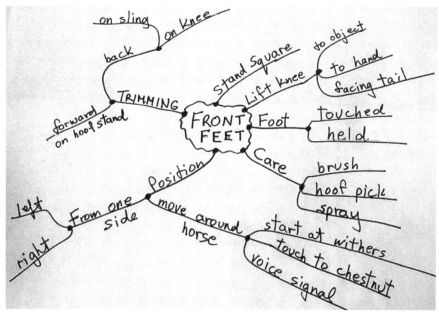

Figure 24: Slices in the process of building confidence about offering the front feet.

Lifting Front Feet for Balance

Conditions:

- at home
- usual handler
- parked on a mat; not tied up.

Using a mat is an excellent way to let our horse know that we want him to stay parked on this spot.

You will notice that in some of the pictures Boots has no rope on and in others she is ground-tied. Sometimes it is convenient to have a rope on. Information about teaching your horse to ground-tie is in Chapter 8 of my book, *How to Create Good Horse Training Plans*. *#72* and *#73 HorseGym with Boots* illustrate the process.

Figure 25: Boots is setting herself up on the mat. Because I've taught duration standing on a mat, using a mat for hoof care lets her know that I'd like her to stay parked on this spot.

Slice 1: Ensure horse is standing squarely

The prerequisite task of stepping forward and backward, one step at a time, ensures that the horse understands our request to stand squarely. It helps if we routinely ask for square halts in a variety of situations. Each square halt, on request, earns a click&treat.

When asking the horse to square up, slightly tilt his head away from the front foot you want him to move. Moving his head away frees up the shoulder so he can move the leg.

If you are asking the horse to step backwards, be mindful that horses step back with the same footfall as their trot forward. In other words, diagonal feet move together. So, if you would like the horse to move a hind foot slightly back, tilt his nose slightly to the same side as the foot you want to move. *#86 HorseGym with Boots* demonstrates.

It took me considerable effort and thoughtfulness to establish how I needed to ask for a specific foot to move forward or back. And it took more application to put it into my long-term memory. If you play with it in a low-key way, both you and the horse will get the hang of it.

Using a mat makes it easier because, as the mat-savvy horse approaches the mat, he knows he will halt with his front feet on the mat. In other words, he has time to mentally and physically prepare himself to halt squarely to earn his click&treat.

#6-#14 HorseGym with Boots go into detail about teaching mats as foot targets.

Slice 2: Knee-lift to touch a target

If we touch a target item gently to the front of the horse's knee, accompanied by a click&treat, most clicker-savvy horses will quickly learn to raise the knee to touch the target if we hold it a little bit above the knee. Start by making sure the horse is standing squarely.

A pool noodle, the end of a dressage whip, a plastic bottle attached to a light stick (e.g. bamboo), or a light stick with bubble wrap taped around it, are the sorts of items we can use for knee targets.

#89 HorseGym with Boots demonstrates.

Figure 26: Teaching the skill of lifting a front foot to touch a target gives a horse ample opportunity to develop balance on three legs. Here I'm on Boots' left side. The mat is an old electric blanket.

Time your click to the moment that the leg is **lifting**. If you click too late, when the leg is on its way down, you're not explaining that the *lift* is what earns the click&treat.

Work equally on both sides. If one side is harder, spend extra time on that side. Like us, horses are right handed or left handed and tend to use one side of their body in preference to the other side. If we make a habit of teaching everything on both sides, it evens out the horse's asymmetry, as well as our own.

Once the horse shows, over several sessions, that he understands the concept, you can add voice and gesture signals as you present the target. If you consistently use a voice signal (e.g. "Lift"), you will build a signal that becomes very handy for many things.

Slice 3: Change to targeting our hand

When it feels right, ask for the leg lift using your hand as a target, rather than an item held in your hand.

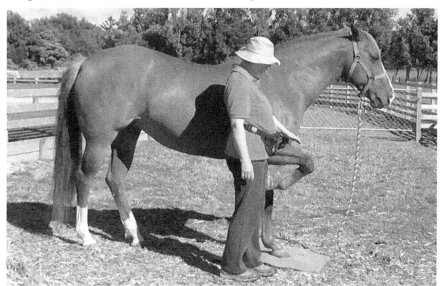

Figure 27: At some point, you'll be able to ask the horse to target your hand rather than an object you are holding. Here I'm on Boots' right side. Note that I did not check she was standing squarely.

Holding a Front Foot

Slice 1: Stand squarely

Ensure that the horse is standing squarely.

Slice 2: Change of body orientation

To hold a front foot for cleaning, inspection or trimming, we orientate our body so we are facing the horse's tail.

We need to be sure that the horse is comfortable with this change in our body's orientation. It's easy to presume our horse won't be bothered, but horses are super sensitive to every small change we make.

It pays to take the time to teach leg-lifting again from scratch when we face the horse's tail.

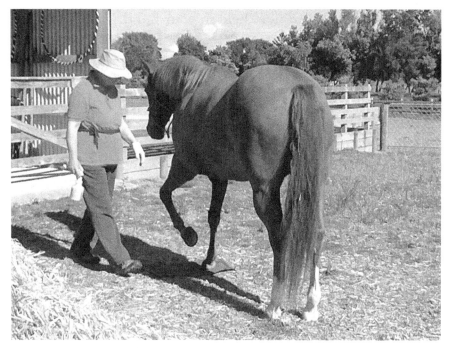

Figure 28: To hold a foot for cleaning and inspection, our body orientation changes to face the horse's tail rather than facing forward. Boots now offers her foot when she sees the hoof-pick and spray bottle in my hand. I'm about to bend over to reach for her foot as it comes up. I'm on her left side.

Slice 3: Hold the foot for longer

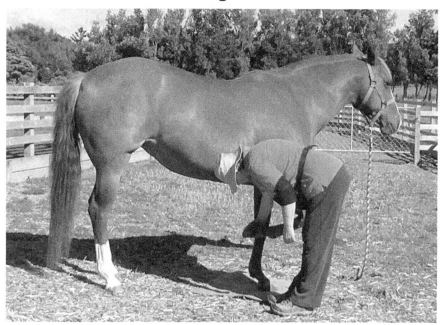

Figure 29: I'm on Boots' right side, holding her foot up with a light hand. If I feel any tension in her body, I release the foot and begin again. We always give the foot back if the horse asks for it. It's easy to reset and start again. You can see from her raised head position that at this moment she is not fully relaxed. She is more anxious when I am on her right side.

Once the horse is relaxed about lifting his foot while we face his tail, we can work on duration of keeping the foot up using the following extra-thin slices.

1. Put your hand on his lifted foot; click, release the foot, relax & deliver a treat.

2. Hold his foot lightly for one second; click during that second, release the foot, relax & deliver a treat.

3. Increase how long you hold the foot, one second at a time. Click just **before** you release the foot; relax and deliver a treat.

4. If you can, click & deliver a treat while holding the foot.

Figure 30: One way to build duration for keeping the foot up is to click&treat while still holding the foot.

If you have a helper who understands clicker training, you can click and have the helper deliver the treat. A helper is especially useful to build duration holding up the hind feet.

As mentioned earlier, when we teach foot care with reward reinforcement, we never hold on to the foot if the horse wants to draw the foot away. We allow him to set it down, pause briefly and ask for it again. In other words, we reset the task each time.

It could be that a horse needs each foot released, whenever he asks for it back, a certain number of times, after which he becomes relatively comfortable about leaving his foot in our hands.

By releasing the foot each time the horse tenses, we allow him the time he needs to overcome the mental fear about having his foot 'trapped'. The number of times he needs his foot returned is probably a function of the depth of his fear.

We must also be aware of the physical aspect. This can be simple discomfort or actual pain. It's not natural to bear all the weight on three legs. A muscle spasm or pinched nerve is highly possible. If we are doing more than a quick clean and inspection, we need to give each foot frequent breaks.

Having the leg pulled sideways, as is the habit of some farriers and trimmers when they trap the foot between their knees is exceedingly uncomfortable. Fortunately, more professionals are now using a hoof sling on which the horse can rest his foot in a more natural and comfortable position.

Slice 4: Foot care procedures

#90 HorseGym with Boots illustrates.

As prerequisites, we have made the horse comfortable with stick-like objects, ropes and brushes. For a horse new to foot care, we might start with a stiff brush to clean off debris, plus a hoof pick to clean out the grooves and corners.

If you live in a damp climate, you may at times want to use a spray of apple cider vinegar to discourage fungal growth called thrush. If a horse develops thrush, a spray of iodine solution deep into the cracks and crevices once a day can clear it up. Some people use a copper sulfate solution or special thrush remedies. Sudocrem, the ointment for nappy (diaper) rash is also known to work, as is tea tree oil.

To introduce a horse to the idea of a spray bottle, fill one with water and walk away with the horse behind you, occasionally spraying the bottle in front of you. He may follow you at liberty or you can have him on a casual rope and ask him to follow you. The following sequence of nine steps seems to work well. *#93 HorseGym with Boots* demonstrates.

1. Walk away with the horse following, spraying water casually. Be aware of wind direction so the spray doesn't waft back toward the horse when you first do this. For this first introduction, another person to walk away doing the spraying can be really helpful. You can follow with the horse at a distance that the horse finds comfortable, keeping a loose lead rope so the horse decides the distance from the spray bottle.

Figure 31: I'm walking away spraying water, giving Boots lots of rope so she can hang back if she is worried.

2. When he is relaxed behind you, <u>turn and walk backwards</u>. Spray the water but not at the horse – spray it sideways.

3. As the horse relaxes and shows interest, walk more slowly so he can get closer. For this slice, you might be able to increase interest by adding something interesting-smelling to the water, such as apple cider vinegar or molasses.

4. When he shows more relaxed interest, halt and quietly keep spraying sideways. When he maintains his interest in the spray bottle, stop spraying and let him sniff it.

Figure 32: I've walked backwards and Boots has indicated that she is ready to sniff the bottle, so I halt and give her time to investigate. After spraying toward the ground a few times, she was able to stand still when I sprayed her shoulder. It was a hot day, so it probably felt nice.

5. Turn the bottle nozzle away from the horse and spray away from him.

6. If he remains calm, do a short, gentle spray on his shoulder; click&treat. If he finds this worrying, go back to earlier steps.

7. Spray a bit more; click&treat.

8. Carry on with a light spray on his shoulder and legs, each one followed by a click&treat.

9. At some point, ask him to pick up a front foot and spray it. Success.

As mentioned above, if the horse is very dubious, maybe put something tasty like molasses into the water and see if you can capture his curiosity so he wants to sniff the bottle.

Some horses will overcome their anxiety over one session. Other horses may need it broken down over a series of short sessions. If the horse is really worried about the spray bottle, spend about three minutes doing whatever he is comfortable with, then leave it for the next session. Start at the first step with each new session, i.e. walking away. As each step becomes ho-hum, add in the next part.

Slice 5: Touch signal for lifting the front feet

Boots has learned to lift her left front foot when she sees me approaching with the hoof pick because I reward this action each time with a click&treat. It is one of the little things that we do together during our daily routine.

However, I also want her to know signals to lift a foot for me any time and when I don't have a treat handy or when I'm wearing bulky gloves. As our signal, I've chosen a touch to the chestnut, which is inside and a little above the knee.

Figure 33: The chestnut is on the inside of the front leg, just above the knee.

No one is sure about the purpose of the chestnuts. Some say they resemble the scent dispersal organ of other animals. Horses have them on all four legs or just on the front legs.

The chestnuts on the hind legs are on the inside of the leg below the hocks.

One story says that if you peel off a piece of loose chestnut and put it in your pocket, horses will find you very interesting.

When your horse clearly understands the 'lift' voice signal, you can touch or tap the chestnut and use your voice signal at the same time.

Horses, like the rest of us, like to know what is happening before it happens. We can give the horse time to prepare to lift a foot if we always start our request with our hand on the horse's withers. Then we run our hand from the withers down to the chestnut of the leg we want to lift.

In the following picture, Boots is parked on a mat and she is ground-tied. As mentioned earlier, we taught both these skills as important prerequisites to relaxed, comfortable foot care. *#72* and *#73 HorseGym with Boots* look at teaching ground tying.

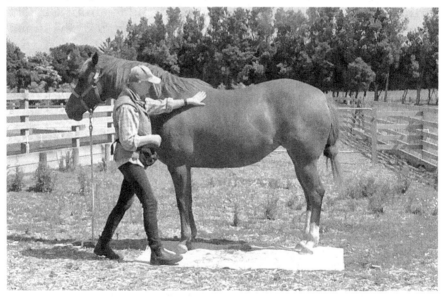

Figure 34: Bridget lets Boots know that she is going to ask for a leg lift by running her hand from Boots' withers down to the chestnut of the front left leg. Note that she's made sure Boots is standing squarely before she starts.

First click&treat when the horse shifts his weight off the leg. Then say your voice signal and tap the chestnut until the horse lifts his foot off the ground, even just a tiny bit; click&treat.

With repeated short sessions, the horse will recognize your voice signal along with your body orientation and the touch on the chestnut.

When you can see that he understands the touch signal well, occasionally ask for a foot this way without adding the click&treat. Use happy praise instead, and rubbing, if your horse likes rubbing.

Clean both front feet from one side

When the horse understands the voice and chestnut touch signal, we can teach the art of cleaning both front feet from one side.

I start with my hand on the withers, then rub it across her girth area so I can tap the chestnut on the far front leg. The horse may be a bit bewildered about this the first few times. But if we do it regularly, rewarded with click&treat, it soon becomes a habit. The horse easily accepts it as part of a regular routine.

We can shape the task with the following click&treat points:

- weight taken off the far front foot
- far front foot lifted slightly
- far front foot held for a moment
- far front leg relaxed enough to allow drawing of the leg back and over behind the near front leg
- duration of holding the far foot increased in one second intervals
- far foot held up in a relaxed manner long enough to clean it out.

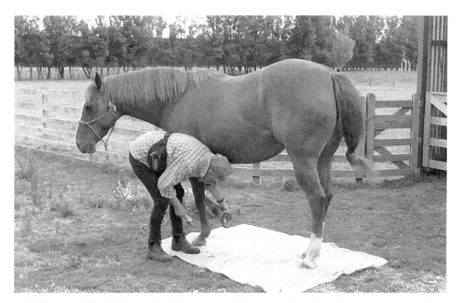

Figure 35: When the horse understands the chestnut touch signal, we can clean both feet from one side. Draw the far foot a little bit toward you <u>behind</u> the near front foot.

I clean feet most days, so doing them all from one side makes it quicker. As I'm right-handed, it is easier for me to be on the horse's left side. *#91 HorseGym with Boots* illustrates.

Trimming Tasks

1. Resting a front foot in a sling

For trimming, it can be helpful if the horse has learned to rest his foot comfortably upside-down on a stand or sling.

To begin, I lay the foot into the sling and hold it there, click and reach my arm back to deliver the treat.

Gradually, I let go of the foot; click&treat. Then it is a matter of building up duration of the foot in the sling one second at a time.

#92 HorseGym with Boots illustrates.

Figure 36: Eventually, the horse will be comfortable leaving the foot in the sling long enough so you can deliver the treat by walking forward to the horse's head.

An option when trimming Boots' front feet is to sit on a low stool and rest her foot on my knee. Some people use a low stool on wheels so they can adjust their position more easily.

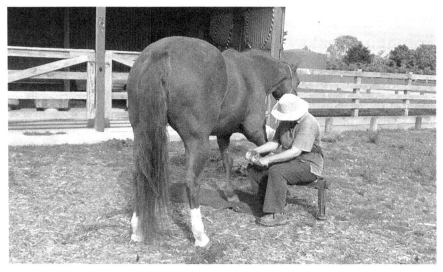

Figure 37: For trimming I often sit on a low stool and rest a front foot on my knee.

2. Bringing a front foot forward onto a hoof stand

We want the horse relaxed about bringing his front foot forward onto a hoof stand so he is ready for this part of a farrier's work. If we keep our own horse trimmed, this is the position we use to put a tidy roll on the front of the hoof wall to avoid chipping.

If you used a stump to teach the horse to lift one front foot, as suggested in the prerequisites, you could put the hoof stand beside the stump, making it easier for the horse to generalize the concept of his hoof up on a stand.

For cleaning the foot, our body orientation had us facing the horse's tail. Now we want the horse to lift a front foot while we are facing forward, allow us to lift the leg and pull it forward so we can place it on the hoof stand.

After making sure the horse is standing squarely, place the hoof stand directly in front of the relevant foot and out as far as the horse's jaw. Generally, this leads to a relatively comfortable stretch for the horse and the foot is flat on the stand.

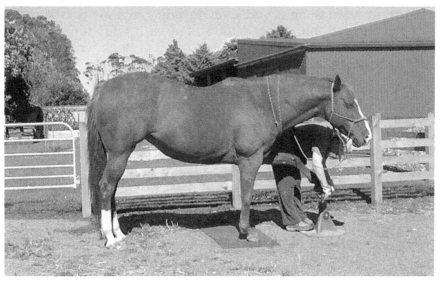

Figure 38: Boots is comfortable with her front foot on a hoof stand. I keep her feet in shape using just a rasp and a hoof knife every week or so.

This is where the prerequisite work with mats, pedestals, stumps, hula hoops, rails, and targeting the knee to our hand all come into play.

We can help our horse a great deal by carefully teaching him the act of keeping his foot on a stand. Before purchasing a hoof stand, I used the bottom of an umbrella stand with a plastic bottle upside-down at the top of the stand, to make it more comfortable for the horse's feet.

If you have someone else trim, your horse usually has little trouble generalizing your teaching with a stump, rock or a block of wood, to the farrier's hoof stand.

By teaching this skill slowly, in your own time, over many short sessions, your horse can avoid the trauma of sudden abrupt foot handling by a stranger. If the horse already understands the process, you've done a great deal to overcome his anxiety. Most professional farriers or trimmers will be only too happy to have your horse offer to put his foot on a hoof stand.

It makes sense to discuss how you do things with any farrier or trimmer that you hire. At times, it can be to the horse's long term advantage if you offer to pay extra for the trimmer to spend extra time to get acquainted with your horse and to take his time, allowing your horse his foot back whenever the horse requests it back.

If you ask for a double time slot at the beginning, you have more chance of staying in control of what is happening with your horse.

Chapter 6: Hind Foot Behaviors

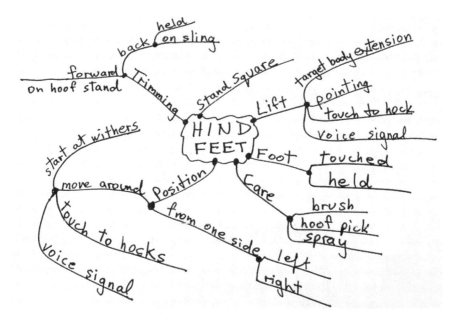

Figure 39: Mind map showing the key slices for building confidence to yield the hind feet to our hands.

Lifting the Hind Feet for Balance

Conditions:

- at home in usual spot
- on a mat
- usual handler
- after achieving front foot confidence.

When the horse is comfortable picking up the front legs on request, we can proceed in a similar way with the hind legs.

We start with making sure the horse is comfortable being rubbed all over with a body extension, paying special attention to the belly and hind legs. *#87 HorseGym with Boots* demonstrates.

If the horse expresses concern about being touched with a body extension or with having a rope swung lightly around his hind legs, we've found a big training hole.

It's essential to go back and build the horse's confidence about standing still while we do things around him. #20 *HorseGym with Boots* looks at *The Art of Standing Still*.

Slice 1: Leg touch confidence

Before we proceed with picking up feet, we need the horse calm and relaxed having his legs brushed with a soft brush right down to his feet. We want him to remain calm and relaxed when we rub and massage his legs all the way down.

Figure 40: By using a body extension, we can ensure that the horse is comfortable being touched all over his legs while keeping our own body fairly upright and out of the kick zone. Smoky has his ear and eye on what Bridget is doing, but overall his tail and body are relaxed.

Slice 2: Touch cap of hock with body extension

My touch signal for picking up a hind foot is to tap the cap of the hock, so that's where I start. I touch the horse with a soft target like a pool noodle, or tickle him there with the end of a dressage whip.

Figure 41: To develop the idea of lifting a hind leg on signal, we can touch the hock gently with a target stick or hold it above the hock so the horse targets it with his hock. Be sure to click as the leg is coming up, not on its way down. Bridget is using a plastic tomato stake with bubble wrap around it.

#89 HorseGym with Boots illustrates.

Here are the key click points:

- first shift of weight off that foot
- slightest lift of foot
- larger lift of leg.

Stay with each click point until the horse does it calmly. The horse's response may be good one day but sticky again the next day. A series of quiet repeats, done as often as possible, will make it smooth and reliable. Once the horse understands what earns the click&treat, add in your voice signal.

Again, be sure to click while the leg is moving up. If you find you are clicking too late, practice bouncing a ball, clicking as the ball comes up off the ground. Repeat this several times a day, over several days. Your timing and your eye-hand coordination will improve.

Figure 42: This is the moment of upward movement that we want to click&treat. If the foot is on its way down, we have missed the moment. Once the horse understands, add your voice signal.

Slice 3: Change to pointing

As with the front feet, it will eventually feel right to phase out the body extension and instead use a pointing gesture to ask for the hind foot to lift. Remember to use your voice signal as well. It will help the horse respond consistently to your pointing signal.

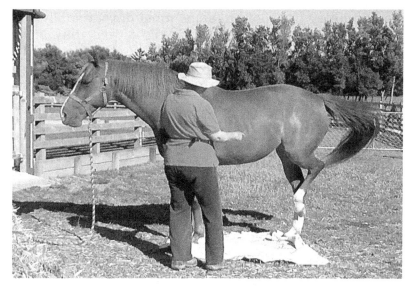

Figure 43: Once the horse understands the request, a pointed finger replaces the body extension. Here I am on her left side.

Once the horse understands the point and voice signals, he will usually generalize his response to another trusted person who uses the same signals.

Figure 44: Once the horse understands the pointing gesture and the voice "Lift" signal, he will usually generalize it to other trusted handlers.

Boots and I play the 'foot lift' game most days, usually as one of our *end of session* activities. Doing it every day keeps it fresh in our repertoire. It sustains the horse's ability to balance cleanly on each different set of three legs. *#89 HorseGym with Boots* demonstrates.

Holding the Hind Feet

Slice 1: Stand squarely

Check that the horse is standing squarely. After a while, you'll do this automatically as part of the task. Teach the hind foot skills in your usual foot care spot with the horse parked on a familiar mat.

Slice 2: From withers to cap of hock

Start with your hand at the withers and run it along the horse's back, down his butt and touch the cap of his hock; click and promptly move to the front of the horse to deliver the treat. We don't want him to swing his head around or move his feet looking for the treat.

#90 HorseGym with Boots illustrates.

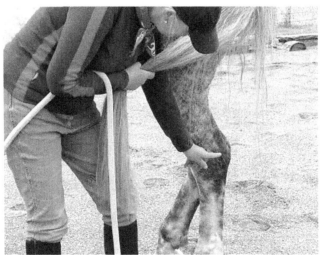

Figure 45: The cap of the hock is a handy spot for teaching a touch signal to lift a hind leg.

Gradually work through a series of mini-slices as outlined below. Stay with each mini-slice until it feels comfortable for you and ho-hum for the horse. A horse tells us when something is ho-hum by keeping his neck low with his ears at or below the withers and his overall body has an aura of relaxation. His ears are floppy and his lower lip is loose.

There is no point moving on to the third mini-slice if the horse is not standing squarely and totally comfortable with your hand moving from his withers to his hock.

We are working close to the horse, so we can easily differentiate between the feel of a horse with tense muscles and one who is standing calmly. Whenever you feel muscle tension, release the leg, stand back a bit, relax and breathe deeply. Then start again.

The mini-slices:

1. Make sure the horse is standing squarely.

2. Run your hand from withers to hock; click&treat. Repeat until you are sure the horse is relaxed with this. As mentioned earlier, move promptly to the front of the horse to deliver the treat so he learns that he doesn't have to swing his neck around or move his feet to get the treat.

3. Tap his hock and use your voice "Lift" signal. Click&treat for the slightest shift of his weight off that foot.

4. If the horse is reluctant to lift his foot, spend more time teaching the voice signal while tapping his hock with a soft body extension (Figures 41 and 42) and with the pointing game. Use the voice signal each time to establish it strongly.

The main benefit of slowly running our hand from withers to hock is that it consistently gives the horse time to shift his weight off the leg that we want to pick up.

Figure 46: Boots is in the process of shifting her weight so she can lift her left hind leg. The arrow points to her front right foot which is changing position while she shifts her weight.

5. As we did with the front feet, the next mini-slice is to put our hand on the foot; click, release the foot and deliver the treat.

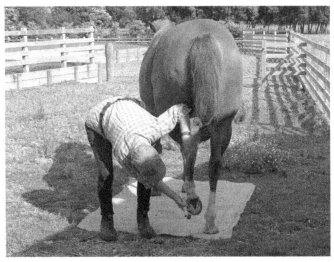

Figure 47: After Boots lifts her foot, Bridget holds it lightly and clicks before she releases the foot and moves to Boots' head to deliver the treat. The click&treat is for the lifting of the foot.

6. Gradually hold the foot up for longer. Take your time with this. Feel the horse's muscle tension/relaxation. The instant you feel tension, release the foot, stand up, take your energy away from the horse and take a few deep breaths. <u>Don't click&treat</u>.

The only time you click&treat is if the horse is still relaxed with his foot <u>up</u>. Work on duration in one second increments. Don't ask for two seconds until you get at least 10 relaxed 'holds' of one second duration over several sessions.

It will definitely feel like paint drying, but taking the time now will allow the horse to work through the natural fear he feels when a foot is compromised. If we don't allow him the time he needs to build his confidence, he can't bring the foot care process inside his comfort zone.

I think horses are often more anxious about their hind feet because many predators dodge in to hamstring a hind leg, then follow until the horse is too weak and sore to escape the kill.

Figure 48: The quickest way to calm, comfortable care of the hind feet is to take as long as it takes for the horse to overcome his instinctive fear about having a hind leg compromised.

As mentioned earlier, the horse may have a significantly different emotional response to each foot.

Quite a few horses seem most anxious about the right hind leg. This could be because we usually do more things on the horse's left side, making him more comfortable with a handler on that side. Since most people are right-handed, it's also harder for us to get smooth picking up feet on the horse's right side.

At some point, you will know that it's time to introduce a brush and hoof pick to clean out the feet.

There is usually no need to pull the horse's feet up and out great distances. The more comfortable we can keep him, the quicker he will be able to overcome his anxiety.

Cleaning both hind feet from one side

Once the horse understands the voice and hock touch signals for lifting a hind foot on request, we can introduce the idea of cleaning the hind feet staying on one side of the horse. *#91 HorseGym with Boots* demonstrates.

Figure 49: Bridget is on Boots' left side. She started at the withers, ran her hand across the butt under the tail to the far side so she could tap Boots' right hock to ask for the leg to lift. Then she quietly waits for Boots to relax her leg so she can draw it over <u>behind</u> the near hind leg.

To build the skill we can shape the task with the following click&treat points:

- weight taken off the far hind foot
- far hind foot lifted slightly
- far hind foot held for a moment
- far hind leg relaxed enough to allow drawing of leg back and over
- duration of holding far foot increased in one second intervals
- far foot held up in a relaxed manner long enough to clean it out

Trimming Tasks

1. Resting the hind foot in a sling

#92 HorseGym with Boots demonstrates.

Teaching the horse to rest his hind foot in a sling helps him prepare for trimming, whether you do it yourself or have a farrier or barefoot trimmer.

It will take experimentation to work out just where to position the sling to make it as comfortable as possible for the horse.

The position of the sling at its lowest setting on my hoof jack is higher than I hold Boots' foot when I trim, so it is a new experience for her.

Even if I don't use it regularly, it can be a handy skill to have when the bottom of the foot needs attention.

Figure 50: This photo is from an early lesson about resting a hind foot in a sling. Boots is not yet totally relaxed with his position because I don't use this tool on a regular basis.

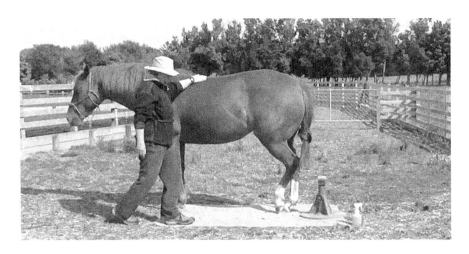

Figure 51: As before, I let Boots know that I am about to ask for her hind foot by running my hand from her withers to her hock. She has already shifted her weight off the left hind leg.

Figure 52: You can see that we are still working on duration, i.e. keeping the hind foot resting on the sling. Boots is in the act of pulling her foot off the sling. For this 'duration building' part of the training, it can be helpful to have a helper at the front of the horse to offer the treat while you click and stay with the back of the horse.

2. Bringing the hind foot forward onto a hoof stand

We want the horse relaxed about bringing his hind foot forward onto a hoof stand for part of a farrier's work, or so we can round off the front of the hoof wall to avoid chipping.

Figure 53: When beginning work with the hind feet, it can make it easier to have a helper deliver the treat when you click. Be sure they know how to deliver the treat promptly in a firm flat hand.

As mentioned earlier, we want to build the horse's confidence in tiny increments that keep him being successful (i.e. earning a click&treat) as much as possible.

In other words, we want as high a rate of reinforcement as possible at the beginning. If the horse expresses a need to put his foot down, <u>we should always release it</u>, pause momentarily, then begin again.

It's important that we retain our emotional neutrality while the horse is working through these difficult skills. If we get anxious or frustrated, the horse will immediately pick up on our discomfort and become more concerned about the whole procedure.

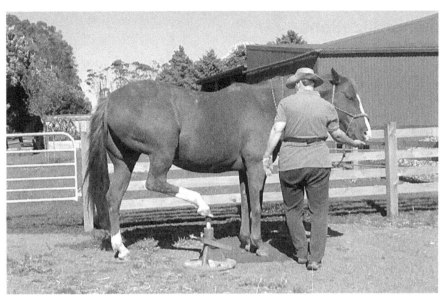

Figure 54: If you gradually build duration, you will soon be able to ask the horse to leave his foot up while you move to his head to deliver the treat.

Figure 55: To save my back, I teach a signal for the horse to move his foot off the stand. I'm touching her lightly on the chests, saying "Back". I have my foot on the stand to stop it tipping over as she drags her foot back. I <u>don't</u> click&treat.

Generalizations

When it's all working smoothly in your usual foot care spot, you can generalize by:

- moving a familiar mat to new places
- use the familiar place, but no mat
- ask for a foot in novel situations.

Conclusion

That brings us to the end of the teaching and learning sequences to help a horse and handler toward stress-free foot care.

Hopefully, it has provided ideas that you can apply to the concept of 'move closer, stay longer'. At first you may not feel comfortable getting very close or staying very long. Rest assured that the horse has more anxiety than the handler.

Your starting point is always something that you and the horse can already do. The end point is relaxed foot care in a variety of situations. In-between are the activities outlined in the book.

Checklist

No.	DETAILS	Tick
	Prerequisites	
1	Handler & horse are clicker-savvy	
2	Leads easily, halts promptly & backs up readily	
3	Horse can park & be rubbed all over	
4	Foot awareness with mats & other exercises	
5	Brush legs	
6	Rub legs with hands	
7	Comfortable 'foot care' spot sorted	
8	Stand squarely	
	Major Slices for Building Front Foot Behaviors	
1	Lift knee to target an object: click for foot rising	
2	Lifts knee to hand	
3	Add in consistent voice signal	
4	Handler faces tail to ask for leg to target hand	
5	Catch & hold foot briefly: click <u>before</u> releasing	
6	Hold foot for one second	
7	Hold foot for two seconds	

8	Gradually hold foot longer, one second at a time	
9	Clean foot with stiff brush	
10	Clean foot with hoof pick	
11	Teach spray bottle confidence	
12	Set foot in sling (or on knee)	
13	Build duration of foot in sling or on knee	
14	Bring foot forward onto a hoof stand or stump	
15	Build duration of hoof brought forward	
16	Back foot off hoof stand (no click&treat, just praise)	
Major Slices for Building Hind Foot Behaviors		
1	Confident with body extension rubbed over legs	
2	Confident with brush and hands rubbing legs	
3	Touch cap of hock with body extension for lift	
4	Add voice signal	
5	Lift hind foot with pointing	
6	Run hand from withers to cap of hock – relaxed	
7	Lifts foot with tap on hock & voice signal	
8	Hold foot briefly; click; go to head to give treat	
9	Hold foot one second; click; go to head to treat	

10	Hold foot two seconds; click; go to head to treat	
11	Gradually hold foot longer one second at a time	
12	Clean hoof with brush	
13	Clean hoof with hoof pick	
14	Spray hoof	
15	Clean both hind feet from one side	
16	Rest hind foot in a sling	
17	Bring hind foot forward onto a hoof stand	
18	Build duration on the hoof stand	
19	Teach 'back' signal for foot off stand (no click&treat)	
	Generalizations	
1	Familiar mat in new spots	
2	Familiar spot without mat	
3	New spots without mat	
4	Away from home	

Acknowledgements

As always, my appreciation for my editors, Colleen Spence in Canada and Larry Metcalf in the USA knows no bounds.

And writing these books would not be nearly as much fun without the input of Bridget Evans. She is not only a superb critic of my more rampant flights of fancy, she is also a great friend and willingly gives up days at a time to come and play with Boots and me.

Figure 56: Bridget and Boots waiting in 'protected contact' for filming of a video clip about how to get started with clicker training. Boots watched while Bridget modelled the behavior we wanted from the horse.

Appendix 1: Starting Clicker Training

Materials: Gear Checklist

1. A **training venue** where the horse feels comfortable. Ideally, his herd buddies are in view but not able to interfere.
2. The horse behind a **safe barrier**. This could be a non-wire fence or a gate or stall guard.

Figure 1: When starting a horse off with clicker training, it's wise to use protected contact, which just means keeping a barrier between you and the horse until you have established good table manners. Sometimes your only safe option might be to tie the horse up as in Figure 2. Protected contact allows you to step out of reach if the horse becomes over-enthusiastic.

Figure 2: Sometimes our only safe option is to have the horse tied up. Tying up with a wide halter is safer than tying with a rope halter in case something causes the horse to pull back. We're also using a Blocker Tie Ring. If the horse pulls back, there will be friction on the rope, but the rope can pull free completely, so the horse's whole weight won't be impacting the sensitive neck vertebrae.

You can find out more about the Blocker tie ring at: http://blockerranch.com/.

If the horse is tied up, make sure that he is able to relax when he is tied and that you allow him enough rope so he can easily engage with the target.

Protected contact allows you to stay safe if the horse becomes overly keen or excited about the idea of earning a tasty treat. You won't know how he will react until you try it out.

3. Decide on your **marker sound**; organize your mechanical clicker if you intend to use one. Having it on a cord around your neck or wrist means you can let go of it when you need to use your hand. But it also means you have to get it ready before you want to use it again so the timing of your click is accurate. I use a mechanical clicker sometimes to teach something new, but most of the time I use a tongue click. If you can't make a clear tongue click sound, a special short, sharp

word or sound (not used any other time) works just as well. For simplicity in these notes, I'll use the word 'click' to refer to whatever marker sound you decide to use.

4. You need a **pouch or pocket** that easily lets your hand slip in and out. One of my favourites is a hoodie-style sweatshirt with a continuous front pocket that allows me easy access to the treats with either hand. Mostly I use a bum bag (fanny pack) type pouch.

5. The **treats**: people use tiny portions of carrot, apple, celery, grain, horse nuts, cereal, crackers, dry bread, rice cakes, popped popcorn — anything your horse likes. Individual pieces are often easier to manage than loose grain. Casual experimentation lets you find out which treats your horse likes best. My horse loves peppermints, so we use these for very special occasions like a superb response when we are learning something new. Often, I have a variety of treats. Apple pieces score higher with my horse than carrot pieces.

Figure 3: It doesn't take long to get into the habit of getting the treats ready before heading out to our horse.

6. You can **count out a specific number of treats** for a short training session or just have an abundant treat supply at hand. Running out of treats during a session is not helpful for the horse. I usually have spare horse pellets handy in a sealed container in case I need more.

7. You need a **hand-held target** to teach the horse that he has to *physically do something* (e.g. touch his nose to the target) in order to earn the click&treat. It's easiest to start with a target on a stick. A plastic drink bottle taped to a stick makes a nice safe, lightweight target. If the horse is nervous of sticks due to past experiences, a plastic bottle by itself, as in Figure 4 may be a better way to start. Some people use a fly swatter.

8. Ensure that the horse is **not hungry**. We want the horse to be interested, but not over-excited by the idea of special food coming his way.

9. If your horse is on restricted calories, ensure that his treats are counted as part of his daily total.

Two Extra Points

1. If the horse is wary about a new object like a target on a stick or a plastic bottle, I like to walk away backwards with the object (or have a helper walk away backwards with it while the horse and I follow together), and encourage the horse to follow until he makes up his own mind that it is okay to put his nose near or on the new item. Horses tend to follow things moving away and retreat from things moving toward them.

2. If you click by mistake, it's best to deliver the treat anyway. At this point you are training to give meaning to the click, so this is important. We want *the click and the treat* to belong together in the horse's mind.

Method

1. Simulation: Giving Meaning to the Click

It's ideal to learn the process of giving meaning to the click with a person standing in for the horse. The more adept we are with the mechanics of treat delivery before heading out to the horse, the more our horse will buy into our confidence that we know what we are doing.

1. Have your hand ready on the clicker (if using a clicker).

2. Present the target a little bit away from the person, so he or she has to reach toward it to touch it.

Figure 4: Learning the mechanics of the process with another person standing in for the horse means that the horse doesn't have to put up with our first fumbling as we work it all out. We have to get our head and our muscle memory around how to carry out the routine smoothly. If we approach the horse confident with what we are doing, the horse will buy into our confidence. I have the clicker in the same hand as the bottle so my other hand is free to deal with the treats.

3. *Wait* for the person to touch the target with their hand (be patient).
4. The instant they touch it, click or say your chosen word or sound.
5. Lower the target down and behind your body to take it out of play.
6. Reach into your pocket/pouch for the treat (maybe use coins or bits of cardboard or mini chocolates).
7. Extend your arm fully to deliver the treat.
8. Stretch your treat hand out flat so it is like a dinner plate with the treat on it.
9. Hold your arm and hand firm so your pretend horse can't push it down.
10. When the 'horse' has taken the treat, pause briefly, then begin again with #1.
11. *Ignore* any unwanted behavior as much as possible.
12. Turn a shoulder or move your body/pouch out of reach if the person pretending to be your horse tries to mug you for a treat. Your 'pretend horse' has to learn that he or she earns the click&treat only by touching the target. If your 'pretend horse' is strongly invasive, put a barrier between you.
13. Multiple short sessions (up to 3 minutes long) at different times allow your brain and your muscle memory to absorb the technique, especially the finer points of timing.
14. If your helper is willing, let him or her be the teacher and you take a turn being the horse. Playing with being the horse is often a real eye-opener.

2. With the Horse

A: Giving Meaning to the Click: Touching a Target

The final goal is for the horse to move willingly to follow the target so he can put his nose on it to earn a click&treat.

First Session

1. Count about 20 treats into your pocket/pouch. Have a few spares handy in case you want to finish the session by putting a handful of treats into the horse's food bucket (or on the grass) as an *end of session* signal.

2. Hold the target near his nose, but don't *thrust* it at him.

3. *Wait* until he touches even a whisker to it - *click* and *move the target* out of sight behind you. Moving the target out of sight will encourage his attention to the target when you present it again for the next repeat.

4. As you move the target behind you, simultaneously *reach for the treat* and deliver it away from your body by holding your hand out straight and rotating your shoulder to create a solid platform with your totally flat hand.

Figure 5: Deliver the treat with a flat hand and an outstretched arm so your body is well away from the horse. After the click, I move the target out of sight behind me to 'take it out of play'. It will then be obvious to the horse when I present it again.

5. If using a mechanical clicker, put your hand on the clicker ready to click.

6. Then hold out the target again. In your early sessions, put the target in the same place so you keep it easy for the horse to touch. At some point, you will see that he really *gets* the connection between touching the target, the click, and the treat.

7. Repeat until you've used up your 20 treats. Ignore unwanted behavior. Stop after a good response. A few treats in a feed dish or on the grass is a nice way to let the horse know that one of your mini-sessions is finished. Put the target away out of sight.

8. Lots of short sessions (about 20 treats or 3 minutes) work well. You can do other things with the horse between the mini clicker training sessions.

9. Keep all your 'targeting criteria' the same until you get 10/10 confident repeats in a row, every time, over at least three consecutive sessions.

   By targeting criteria, I mean:
   * where you train
   * where you stand in relation to the horse
   * how and where you present the target.

Create a consistent end of session game that lets the horse know that the clicker training session is about to finish. Boots likes to finish with a series of belly crunches or touching various body parts to my hand. When I actually stop, I use a voice signal, "All gone," along with a gesture made by swinging my arms back and forth across each other at waist level several times. A handful of treats in a food bowl or on the grass is one way to signal that we're finished for now.

To find out more about belly crunches, check out www.Intrinzen.horse.

Part B, coming up shortly, outlines how to make the target more interesting once the horse is totally ho-hum and consistent with touching his nose to the target when you hold it out near his nose.

The clip called *Clicker 1 with Smoky* in my *'Starting Clicker Training'* playlist illustrates the process of teaching the horse the connection between touching the target, the click, and the treat.

B. Lunging for the Treat

Some horses are always polite, others not so.
1. Be safe. Put a barrier between you and the horse so you can move back out of range.
2. Make sure that the horse is **not hungry**. We want the horse interested in clicker work, but not over-excited or aroused by the thought of food treats.
3. Check out your **food delivery** method.
   a) Does it take too long to get your hand into and out of your pocket or pouch? Can you find easier pockets or a more open pouch?
   b) Do you move your hand toward your treats *before* you've clicked? This can cause major problems because the horse will be watching your hand rather than focusing on what you are teaching.
4. Be sure to only feed treats if they have been earned *and you have clicked.* Ask the horse to do something before giving a treat, either have him touch the target or take a step or two backwards.
5. Avoid feeding any treats by hand unless you have asked for a behavior and clicked for it. When not clicker training, put treats in a feed dish or on the grass.
6. Hold your treat hand where you want the horse to be rather than where he has stuck his nose. In the beginning, we want him to have his head straight to

retrieve the treat. If he is over-eager, it can help to hold the treat toward his chest so he has to shift backwards to receive it.

Figure 6: Boots reached across the fence to put her nose on the target. Now I am showing her that she needs to back up to receive the treat by holding it toward her chest.

7. If he lunges at your treat hand, take hold of the side of his halter after the click, so you have some control of where he puts his mouth. I also use a loud sharp, "Uh" (as in 'up') sound as a warning that the shark-like behavior is not what I'm after.

8. It can help to run your closed treat hand down the horse's nose from above, and ask him to target your fist before you open your hand so he can retrieve the treat.

9. It may also work to bring your fist (closed around the treat) up under his chin and have him target your fist before you flatten your hand so he can retrieve the treat. Often one of these little intervening steps can help build the habit of polite treat-taking.

10. A bit of experimentation will show you what works best with a particular horse.
11. If the horse is over-keen, try using treats that he doesn't consider quite so yummy.
12. With consistency and patience on the handler's part, over-enthusiastic treat-taking usually improves once the horse understands that a click&treat only follows when he carries out a request you have made. He'll learn that a treat will only follow if there has been a click first. That is why we have to be consistent.
13. The horse's character type and current emotional state will influence how he takes the treat.
14. Prompt, cleanly executed treat delivery is always important. Inconsistency and sloppy treat delivery are the first items to look at if things are not going smoothly.

The clip called *Table Manners for Clicker Training* in my *Starting Clicker Training* playlist illustrates how we can use the timing of the click to improve the politeness around treat-retrieval. The clip shows Smoky early in his clicker training education and Zoe who had never done it before.

The method shown on the clip can be improved by not waiting so long to click&treat again. At first, it's good to click&treat often while the horse remains facing forward.

In some parts of the clip we waited for Smoky to turn toward Zoe and then turn away again before she clicked. That runs the risk of having the horse think that turning toward the handler first is part of what we want him to do.

C: Targeting: next sessions

#2 HorseGym with Boots shows the process in action. I would improve the technique shown in the clip by withdrawing the target down behind me, rather than over my shoulder, and standing rather than sitting. Also, not all horses are comfortable working across electric fencing, even if it is not electrified.

1. Once the horse is confidently touching the target held near his nose and seldom loses focus, gradually change the position of the target to make it more challenging for him. Chose one of: higher, lower, to the right, to the left. Teach him each of these one at a time. Each change you make is a big deal for the horse.

2. When he moves his neck to follow the target willingly and with interest, ask him to move a step to the right or the left to reach it. Stay with one direction until he is superb at it, then teach the other direction.

3. When he happily moves one step, gradually build up more steps. You can still be on the other side of a barrier while you teach this.

5. Whenever you change a criterion, begin by clicking for even the smallest hint of behavior heading in the new direction, until the horse shows confidence with the change. Then start withholding the click to gradually get more of what you want.

6. If he gets confused, *always be ready to backtrack* to the place where he can be continuously successful. This is the key to overall success and rapid progress. If he gives up because it's too hard, you have lost his willingness.

7. Stop each session on a high. Horses think about these things overnight. Stopping on a good note helps his motivation to do it again next time. Our tendency is to see if the horse can do it again right away, so we have to remind ourselves to stop right after the best response.

8. When you feel safe, work without the barrier.

9. Get creative to see where he'll happily follow the target (toward, over, between, into and around things).

D. Destination Training

Once the horse understands nose targets, we can hang them around our training area and use them to teach the wonderful habits of a willing 'walk on' and a prompt 'halt'. It operates equally well with ground-work or riding.

Each target becomes a destination that the horse understands. Walking between destinations becomes interesting for the horse because there is always a positive consequence (click&treat) upon reaching the next target.

A clicker-savvy horse soon appreciates the fact that we know the way to the next destination that will earn him a pause and a click&treat. It gives him a reason to want to go where we want to go.

If a horse is barn or buddy-sweet, we can put out targets to gradually build confidence with moving a bit further away. At some point, the horse's thoughts will be more on seeking out the next target than on his buddies, barn or paddock left behind.

It may seem like a lot of effort at first, but once we have gained the horse's confidence about willingly going out and about with us, we can gradually reduce and then phase out the target props. We can use environmental markers (trees, corners, nice grazing spots) instead.

#3 - #5 HorseGym with Boots (inclusive) demonstrate ways of using nose targets in different contexts.

As well as nose targets, we can teach the horse about foot targets using small boards or mats or something like a Frisbee. We can use these as parking spots.

#6 - #18 HorseGym with Boots (inclusive) deal mainly with foot targets.

Figure 7: Boots is coming to a square halt on the mat. Each halt on a mat earns a click&treat so it doesn't take long for the horse to keenly move between mats.

We can set out mats as destinations or we can use something like a Frisbee or an old cap to toss ahead of us, move forward to target it, toss it again, and so on. It's another way we can teach him confidence about leaving his home area. We create an activity that gives him something positive to do.

Figure 8: Bridge has tossed a Frisbee ahead and Boots is keen to follow it to earn her next click&treat.

Providing destinations for my horses was a real breakthrough in how fast they learned and how willingly they applied themselves to learning new tasks that required moving from point A to point B.

Conclusion

For people who have never explored equine clicker training, using a nose target is a great way to start because when you no longer want to do it, you simply put the target away.

Once you get in the habit of having treats with you, and your horse becomes clicker-savvy, you may be tempted to use the mark and reward clicker training system to teach your horse other new things or to refine tasks that the horse already knows.

Working for a food reward (even such tiny ones) activates one of the most powerful seeking systems in the deepest part of the brain.

Of course, horses learn readily by seeking out what will *release* signal pressure, i.e. the discomfort-comfort dynamic.

But the motivating factor of a food *reward* allows us to add a whole new dimension to our training. The horse can become proactive in his communication with us. It's also a lot more fun to work with.

Once they are clicker-savvy, horses show a strong desire to work for a food reward. They love the click&treat dynamic because the click (or special word/sound) can be timed to tell them exactly what they did that will earn the treat. Horses love clarity. They like to be right in the same way as we like to be right.

The mark and reward (clicker training) system removes much of the guess-work the horse is faced with when we use only the release reinforcement system.

Most horse-human dysfunction is due to lack of clarity coming from the human side of the relationship for these reasons.

1. Our behavior around the horse is inconsistent.
2. Our signals to ask the horse to do something are inconsistent and/or poorly taught.
3. We are not able to read the horse's body language well enough to understand what he is saying to us.

Most horses are happy to comply with our requests if we teach what we want carefully and ensure our signals are clear and consistent.

Clicker training has the handler looking for the moments to reward, rather than moments that need correction. As the handler gets better and better at thin-slicing a large task into its smallest teachable parts, it becomes easier and easier for the horse to learn by being continually successful.

We learn to reset a task rather than correct something that did not go as we hoped. This makes a huge difference to how horses perceive their training. Clicker-savvy horses often don't want their sessions to end. The positive vibrations that go with good clicker training make it fun rather than a chore.

As mentioned earlier, equine clicker training gives us a way to let the horse know instantly, by the sound of the marker signal (click), when he is right. It takes away much of the guessing horses have to do as they strive to read our intent.

A great deal more detail is available in my book, *How to Begin Equine Clicker Training: Improve Horse-Human Communication.*

Appendix 2: YouTube Video Clips

Most of the video clips are shorter than five minutes, so they are quick to watch and easy to review if you are interested in specific tasks.

To reach my channel, put *Hertha MuddyHorse* into the YouTube search engine. The Clips are in one of three playlists.

1. Most of the clips are in my *HorseGym with Boots* playlist. Each title is written as *#? HorseGym with Boots*. For example, if you want to quickly find Clip number 22, simply put: *#22 HorseGym with Boots* into the YouTube search engine and it should come right up.
2. Some clips are in the *Free-Shaping Examples* playlist. These are named only, so to find a particular clip, go to that playlist and scroll down for the clip's name.
3. Other clips are in the *Thin-Slicing Examples* playlist. These are also only named, so you search the playlist for the title you want.

A list of all the current *HorseGym with Boots* Clips follows, as well as titles in the *Free-Shaping* and *Thin-Slicing* examples.

HorseGym with Boots Series

Topics are added to this series as they are created.
1. Introduction
2. Giving meaning to the click
3. Stationary nose targets
4. Parking at a nose target (also spooky new things to touch)
5. Putting behavior 'on cue'
6. Foot targets (also, free-shaping new behavior)
7. Backing up from the mat

8. Duration on the mat
9. Putting the mat target 'on cue'
10. Generalizing mats
11. Mat-a-thons
12. Chaining tasks
13. Anthem is new to nose targets (Anthem is a young quarter-horse)
14. Anthem is new to foot targets
15. Parking at a distance
16. The 'triple treat'
17. 'Walk-on' and 'halt' multi-cues
18. Parking out of sight
19. Free-shaping
20. The 'art of standing still'
21. Walk away for confidence (with new things)
22. Rope relaxation
23. Hosing on the mat (recognizing 'click points')
24. Parking commotions
25. Parking with ball commotion
26. *8 Leading Positions* overview
27. Good Backing = Good Leading
28. Leading Position Three (beside neck or shoulder)
29. Leading Position Three with a 'circle of markers'
30. Leading Position Three duration exercise
31. Natural and Educated body language signals
32. Sensitivity to Body language
33. Opportunity, Signals 1
34. Signals 2: Gestures
35. Signals 3: Touch
36. Signals 4: Verbal signals (also environmental signals, horse initiated signals and marker signals)
37. Signals 5: Intent
38. Signals 6: Body Orientation (of handler)
39. Train with a Lane 1
40. Train with a Lane 2
41. Leading Position Seven Clip 1 of 4, in front facing horse
42. Leading Position Seven Clip 2 of 4
43. Leading Position Seven Clip 3 of 4
44. Leading Position Seven Clip 4 of 4

45. Leading Position One: Clip 1 of 2 in front, facing away
46. Leading Position One Clip 2 of 2
47. Leading Position Two (horse's nose stays behind handler's shoulder)
48. Leading Position Eight Clip 1 of 7, Go, Whoa & Back (facing the horse's side)
49. Leading Position Eight Clip 2 of 7, Groom, Saddle, Relax
50. Leading Position Eight Clip 3 of 7, Drive-by Grooming & Mounting Prep
51. Leading Position Eight Clip 4 of 7, Side Step in Motion
52. Leading Position Eight Clip 5 of 7, Yielding Front End & Hind End
53. Leading Position Eight Clip 6 of 7, Side Step from Halt
54. Leading Position Eight Clip 7 of 7, Arc Exercise
55. Leading Positions Four and Five (beside ribs & beside butt)
56. Leading Position Four, Clip 2
57. Leading Position Six Clip 1 of 8, Liberty (behind horse)
58. Leading Position Six Clip 2 of 8, One long rein
59. Leading Position Six Clip 3 of 8, Square of lanes
60. Leading Position Six Clip 4 of 8, Rope Calmness
61. Leading Position Six Clip 5 of 8, Two Long Reins: Circle & Weaving
62. Leading Position Six Clip 6 of 8, 4 Leaf Clover Exercise
63. Leading Position Six Clip 7 of 8, 'Gates', Guided Rein, Obstacles
64. Leading Position Six Clip 8 of 8, Trailer Prep
65. Haltering process (with guided free-shaping)
66. Importance of Clear Signals
67. Prep 1 for Weaving, 90 and 180 degree turns; 'Draw' and 'Drive'
68. Weave Prep 2, 360 degree turns
69. Weave Prep 3, Weave a series of objects
70. Weave Prep 4, Only the horse weaves
71. Weave Prep 5, Curves, Circles, at Liberty
72. Ground-tie Clip 1, Getting Started

73. Ground-tie Clip 2, Another Venue
74. Thin-slicing a Trailer Simulation
75. Quiet Sharing of Time and Place
76. Active Sharing of Time and Place + Greet & Go
77. Claim the Spot
78. Watchfulness First Action
79. Watchfulness Second & Third Actions
80. Guiding from Behind
81. Shadow Me
82. Boomerang Frolic
83. Shadow Me Duration with Clicker Training
84. Shadow Me Using Targets
85. Foot care Prerequisites: Lead, Halt & Back-up
86. Asking for One Step at a Time
87. Stick Relaxation
88. Foot Awareness
89. Standing Square & Balance on Three Legs
90. Asking for Each Foot with Touch Signals
91. Asking for Each Foot from One Side
92. The Hoof Stand and Hoof Sling
93. Spray Bottle Confidence

Thin-Slicing Examples

This playlist includes thin-slicing examples about the following topics. To find a specific clip, go to the *Thin-Slicing Examples* playlist in my channel and scroll down to find the one you want. New clips are added as they are made.

- Tunnel with Boots
- Pool Noodle task
- Head Rocking for Poll Relaxation
- Bottle Bank obstacle
- Zigzag for Horse Agility
- Yield Shoulder into a Turn on the Haunches
- Stepping over rails
- Soft yield to Rein Signals (5 Clips which also have their own Playlist)
- Thin-slice 'The Box' Movement (back, sideways, forward, sideways)
- Backing up

- Rope Texting
- Thin-slicing the 1m board
- Water & Tarp obstacle
- Thin-slice the 'Shadow Me' Game at Liberty
- Free-shape Learning to Ring a Bell

Free-Shaping Examples

This playlist includes clips using the free-shaping technique to teach a task. To find a particular clip, go to the *Free-Shaping Examples* playlist in my channel and scroll down to find the clip you want. Most of these clips show both free-shaping and thin-slicing.
- Table Manners for Clicker Training
- Boots and Bicycle
- Bob meets Bicycle (Bob is a young quarter horse)
- Introduction to a saddle (with Bob, his first meeting with a saddle)
- Head-lowering (2 Clips)
- Clicker 1 with Smoky
- Smoky and Dumb-bell target
- Boots picks up the Dumb-bell
- Free-shape Learning to Ring a Bell

There are also short playlists on specific topics including:
- Thin-slicing the Wagon-wheel obstacle
- Teaching the S-bend
- Soft Yield to Rein Signals (5 clips)
- Hula Hoop Challenges (5 clips)
- Single Obstacle Challenges
- 2012 Horse Agility
- 2014 Horse Agility
- 2015 Horse Agility
- 2016 Horse Agility
- 2017 Horse Agility

Most of the Horse Agility clips have a commentary explaining the tasks and showing where we lost marks.

Reference List

Abrantes, Roger. DVDs (2013). *The 20 Principles all Animal Trainers Must Know.* Tawzer Dog LLC. www.TawzerDog.com

Budiansky, Stephen. (1997). *The Nature of the Horse: Their Evolution, Intelligence and Behavior.* Phoenix; London.

Burns, Stephanie. (2002). *Move Closer Stay Longer.* Parelli Natural Horsemanship; Pagosa Springs, Colorado. (Excellent if you feel nervous around horses.)

Camp, Joe (2011). *Training with Treats: with relationship & basic training locked in, treats can become an excellent way to enhance good communication.* 14 Hands Press; USA.

Dorrance, Bill and Desmond, Leslie. (2001). *True Horsemanship Through Feel.* First Lyons Press; Guilford, CT.

Hanson, Mark. (2011). *Revealing Your Hidden Horse: a revolutionary approach to understanding your horse.* Available via Amazon.

Kurland, Alexandra. www.theclickercenter.com

MacLeay, Jennifer. (2003). *Smart Horse: understanding the science of natural horsemanship.* Blood Horse Publications; Lexington, KY.

Pryor, Karen. (1999). *Don't Shoot the Dog: the new art of teaching and training.* Bantam; New York. (About much more than dogs.)

Pryor, Karen. (2009). *Reaching the Animal Mind: Clicker Training and what it teaches us about all animals.* Scribner; New York.

Pryor, Karen. (2014). *On My Mind: reflections on animal behavior and learning.* Sunshine Books Inc; Waltham, MA.

Schneider, Susan M. (2012). *The Science of Consequences: how they affect genes, change the brain and impact our world.* Prometheus Books; New York.

Information about trimming hooves

Barker, Nic and Sarah Braithwaite (2009). *Feet First: Barefoot Performance & Rehabilitation.* JA Allen; London. (www.rockleyfarm.co.uk – the blog on this site has superb slow motion footage) (www.barefoothorses.co.uk – many more resources listed).

Craig, Monique. (2015). *A Modern Look at the Hoof: Morphology, Measuring, Trimming, Shoeing.* Available via Amazon. Fairly in-depth with lots of statistics.

Crosoer, Debs. (2014). *Hoof Geek Guide: Infection Free Hooves.* Available via Amazon. (www.hoofgeek.com).

Harris, Linda. *TACT: The Anatomically Correct Trim.* (http://thehappyhoof.weebly.com/) Also much useful information on YouTube.

Jackson, Jaime (2002). *Horse Owner's Guide to Natural Hoof Care.* Star Ridge Publishing; Arkansas.

Poss, Paige. (www.ironfreehoof.com)

Ramey, P. (2003). *Making Natural Hoof Care Work for You.* Star Ridge Publications; Arizona.

Sullivan, Cindy. (www.tribeequus.com)

Tierney, Maureen. (2012) *The Hoof Guided Method: truly natural barefoot trimming.* English, Indiana; Amazon.com; (http://www.barefoottrimming.com). Not overly complex and made a lot of sense to me and using her ideas improved my horse's feet.

Index

S

T

Made in the USA
Monee, IL
21 December 2019